Enhancing Graduate Impact in Business and Management, Hospitality, Leisure, Sport, Tourism

A valuable addition to the BMAF/HLST series, Enhancing Graduate Impact *offers practical and honest insights into the efforts taken by higher education colleagues to ensure students on their modules and programmes are prepared for the 'real world' on graduation.*

And there is something for everyone – workplace simulations, placements, volunteering, creative assignments, academic integrity, ethical challenges, 'live' projects, mentoring, workshops, work-related learning – many with resources and templates available in the book or on-line. While it has a subject specific education context, the lessons learned can be applied generically across higher education.

One employer reflects, 'It is not enough now to have a degree; we need to know what else they can do.' These case studies meet this challenge by showing how students can have, and in many cases already have had, impact in society.

Mark Freeman
Associate Professor at the Faculty of Business and Economics
University of Sydney

This book goes beyond a simple, blinkered view of employability, recognising the fact that it is not just limited to getting a 'graduate' job – it is about far more than that.

These case studies show how university staff can look beyond the needs of individual modules not only to help students develop attributes for continuing effectiveness and impact in their future employment, but also to be critically self-aware, to know themselves, and thus to make an active contribution as citizens in their wider communities.

The studies are also truthful evaluations of academic practice from a wide range of sources so, although they may be written in a subject or discipline context, they provide lessons to be learned which can be generally applied. It will be a useful resource especially for early academics and academic developers.

Chris Rust
Professor of Higher Education and
Head of Oxford Centre for Staff & Learning Development
Oxford Brookes University

Edited by Patsy Kemp and Richard Atfield

Enhancing Graduate Impact
in Business and Management
Hospitality
Leisure
Sport
Tourism

Threshold Press

First published 2011 by
Threshold Press Ltd
152 Craven Road
Newbury Berks RG14 5NR
Phone 01635-230272 and fax 01635-44804
email: publish@threshold-press.co.uk
www.threshold-press.co.uk

British Library Cataloguing in Publication Data
A catalogue record for this book is available from the British Library

ISBN 978–1–903152–29–4

Printed in South Wales by MWL Print Group, Pontypool

Every effort has been made to trace the copyright holders and we apologise in
advance for any unintentional omissions. The editors and the publisher would be
pleased to insert the appropriate acknowledgement in any subsequent edition.

The editors

Patsy Kemp has experience of working in education and training across the globe. As
academic developments co-ordinator for the Higher Education Academy Network
for Hospitality, Leisure, Sport & Tourism, she works to support practitioners in
their roles in higher education.

Richard Atfield is assistant director for the Business Management Accountancy and
Finance Subject Centre. He is responsible for facilitating workshops, special interest groups and other learning opportunities, including the 2011 BMAF Conference
on 'Graduates with Impact through Excellence in Business Education'. His career
spans management and workforce development in the NHS and lecturing in the
UK and Hong Kong for Oxford Brookes University. Richard is also adjunct associate professor at the University of Canberra.

Contents

Plate section between pages 82 and 83

Introduction

The 'wicked' problem of enhancing graduate impact

Norman Jackson

Our 'wicked' problem

How teachers prepare people for a lifetime of uncertainty and change, and enable them to work with the ever-increasing complexity of the modern world, is the 'wicked' problem shared by higher education institutions and educators all over the world (Rittel and Webber, 1973). As well as preparing our students for the world we know, if we accept the moral purpose of making a difference to their future lives then we also have a responsibility to prepare them for a lifetime of uncertainty, change, challenge and emergent or self-created opportunity. This means that our graduates must be willing and capable of continually learning so that they can adapt to ever-changing contexts.

In choosing to give this book the title *Enhancing Graduate Impact* the editors are pushing this responsibility even further by encouraging higher education not only to prepare students to survive in this uncertain world, but also to enable them to have a positive effect on the world around them. In deliberately using the word 'impact', attention is being focused on a particular type of effect, namely a *significant*, tangible and visible effect, one in which the cause can be more or less attributed to the actions and influences of an individual or their team.

By framing the book in this way the editors are defining a purpose for a higher education that enables learners to develop themselves in ways that allow them to have a significant effect on the organisations in which they will work or the businesses that they will create. This is a real challenge in a higher education world where learning is largely formal, contrasting with the informal ways in which we learn outside the classroom; a world that values codified knowledge and the skills for abstract (academic) problem-solving rather than the embodied knowledge that comes from doing, a world where learning from experience by reflecting on it is greatly undervalued. So it has been a joy to read the contributions to this volume, and appreciate the many approaches being developed and used by business, management, hospitality, leisure, sport and tourism teachers to facilitate student development to achieve this goal.

Assumptions

There are two significant assumptions underlying *Enhancing Graduate Impact*. The first relates to personal agency to have an impact in the world, particularly the world of work. To have a positive and significant effect, the graduate must have the ability to create that impact. The challenge for teachers, embedded in this assumption, is to discover the combination of knowledge, skills, capabilities, qualities, dispositions and other attributes necessary to have effect in the world, and to create the conditions that enable individual students to develop these attributes and integrate them into their professional identity. One way or another all the contributions to this volume are addressing this assumption, some more explicitly than others. An Australian response to this challenge is reflected in the chapter by Wood (Macquarie University), Daly (University of Canberra) and a large project team from other Australian universities. They use a workshop model to address the development of graduate capabilities and devised teaching and learning resources to cultivate and grade these skills. Morris (Higher Education Academy) explores the link between developing skills for good academic practice and the value of these skills in environments beyond higher education. Later in the book, Robinson and Llewellyn at the University of Leeds argue that the study of ethics, in this case with students of sport and exercise science, contributes to graduate impact by developing a more mature and sophisticated way of thinking than might otherwise be the case.

The second assumption relates to our commitment as teachers, departments and institutions to improve on what we are doing so that our graduates are able to have even more impact on the world than at present. We need to understand the effects of our activities and to make sure that what we try to do in the classroom has a place in the world outside. Again, all the contributors to this volume are addressing the challenge embedded in this assumption and sharing what they have learnt so that others might benefit. Specifically, Goodwin from the University of Leicester shares research carried out in the field of tourism management at the University of Gondar, and discusses the implications of its results and of employer engagement for both Ethiopia and the UK. Pointon at De Monfort University writes persuasively about the need for improvement of the experience of international postgraduate students who come to study in the UK, before, during and after their time of study. Haddock-Millar, a professional doctoral student, invited co-students from the Middlesex University Mentoring Network to give their perspective on how this initiative is creating opportunities for them to develop their personal and professional impact in the workplace.

Three senses of graduate impact

Having an impact requires a context and, in the context of this book, we might appreciate three different senses of impact for graduates according to three different contexts. The first, and most obvious, is having an impact in the academic environment. Here the tangible expression might be the production of an excellent essay or dissertation, the solving of a difficult problem or an outstanding presentation. Impact in the academic environment is very much an individualistic rather than a collaborative phenomenon. It is worth noting that employers judge performance more holistically and over many more performances than we tend to in the academic environment. They also place greater value on individual performance in the context of collaboration so that the collective effort has more impact than the sum of individual efforts.

A second interpretation of impact (the one that this book is mainly about) relates to graduate performance in work contexts that can be related to the disciplinary field of study. Here an individual's impact will be judged in terms of the organisation's business and purposes, the value they bring to established practices and beyond this, their creative invention that adds value by changing what has been done before. In this sense of impact we are concerned with the extent to which an academic programme prepares the students for work in the field, and beyond this helps them to develop in such a way that they are effective and inventive. The conundrum for higher education is that an impact in the academic domain does not automatically transfer into an impact in the work domain. In fact, quite the reverse. I have many examples of students who have underperformed academically becoming excellent performers in the work environment. Motivation, recognition, opportunity, support and encouragement that nurture self-belief and capability are all relevant here.

In the tourism marketing field, Jones and Headley at Leeds Metropolitan University use a structured assessment to marry their need for the measurement of academic achievement to the outside world's need for graduates with confidence and understanding of real life business situations. At the London College of Fashion, Gee and Pickard write about the careful construction of curriculum content to create strong relationships within the fashion industry and opportunities for students to interact with this industry at all stages of their degree. The *Small Changes* programme, described by Nield and Simper at Sheffield Hallam University, sends food and nutrition students into the local community, providing benefits to all concerned as well as learning opportunities and employability skills for the students. Barton and Westwood (University of Strathclyde) take us to the competitive area of the law and preparation of those who wish to become practising solicitors; they explore the work they have done using a virtual learning environment to create the experience of working in a team in a real firm. This allows students to make mistakes and learn lessons, which will give them more confidence and self-knowledge when they start work in the world beyond university.

These three chapters and others, especially perhaps those dealing with volunteering (Anderson and Cameron) give examples of the 'learning from experience by reflecting upon it' mentioned earlier. Many of the curriculum and assessment practices described in this book enable students to gain experience of working situations, and give time and opportunity to reflect on them. Ogilvie and Shaw at Manchester Metropolitan University describe how they have taken advantage of the fact that many undergraduates need to work part-time to support themselves, by creating a work-based learning module that incorporates academic learning with that of the very real working situations students find themselves in.

The ability of a student just graduating to demonstrate that they have the potential to have impact on a business will largely depend on whether the student can demonstrate that they have already performed effectively in one or more work situations, ideally supported by the endorsements of their employer. It therefore makes a great deal of educational sense to help learners demonstrate their capability for employment through curriculum designs that integrate learning in the classroom with learning through work. As mentioned above, several contributions to this volume provide examples of this.

The multiple benefits given by volunteering in sport and exercise science are explored by two of the chapters here. As with Nield and Simper in Sheffield, Anderson (University of Wales Institute, Cardiff) and Cameron (University of Abertay, Dundee) show the value that these initiatives can give to a local community as well as giving students the opportunity to demonstrate their effectiveness in a work situation related to their field of study.

A third understanding of impact relates to graduate performance more generally in fields of work that are not directly connected to the discipline studied. Here graduate impact might also be judged in terms of the excellence of performance in routine and non-routine situations, and the added value the graduate employee brings to an organisation through day-to-day participation in the business of the organisation. But we might also judge graduate impact on the ability and preparedness of graduates to adapt their capabilities to contexts that do not specifically relate to their education and training. Here we might refer back to the development of the will and personal agency to succeed in a world that can be both unforgiving and full of opportunity at the same time.

Rushton, Lahlafi and Stretton at Sheffield Hallam University take the development of information literacy skills as part of this preparedness for success in the outside world; the results of their work have the added benefit of contributing to the first measure of impact mentioned here, that of a positive impact on academic performance. Nixon and Dray from Liverpool John Moores University describe the World of Work (WoW®) programme, which works at both university strategy and at programme level, in partnership with employers. This programme goes beyond the boundaries of subject and discipline; it is meeting the challenge of developing graduates who are self-reflective, articulate and highly employable. Drady (University of Sunderland) and Harvey (Newcastle University) describe how they have helped work-experienced management undergraduates tap into their creativity (and the challenges of assessing this). They discuss how this builds confidence, flexibility, and readiness to adapt to different situations.

Capability to act and have an impact

But the ability to have an impact – to perform and make a difference in these different environments, is by no means a simple and straightforward matter. Capability is at the heart of the idea of being able to make an impact. It is the power or ability to do something combined with the will to do something in a certain way that ultimately determines whether someone makes an impact. Capability is an important concept in education and human development; it refers to 'the various combinations of functionings (beings and doings) that [a] person can achieve.' It also reflects a 'person's freedom to lead one type of life or another … to choose from possible livings' (Sen, 1992: 40). Our capability represents 'the *real opportunity* that we have to accomplish what we value' (Sen, 1992: 31).

The capability to make an impact has a number of significant components. The first is *imagination*. An individual has to have the ability to comprehend a situation, to think with sufficient complexity to deal with it and to imagine what might be. How academia nurtures rather than stifles imagination is a critical question for higher education.

The second component of capability is *will*. Without the will to try, even if you don't succeed, nothing is possible. Graduates have to be willing to put themselves into a situation and where necessary to create new situations. Belief in self and one's own capacity and ability to effect a change or make a difference is an integral part of willingness to try. How educators nurture personal will in an environment that seeks compliance with its own will is another difficult challenge for higher education.

The third dimension is *ability*. Knowing that you are able to do something in order to deal with a situation also feeds into your preparedness to try. Students need to develop practical skill, and knowledge of how and when to use that skill in an appropriate manner, to turn ideas into effective action: action that will one way or another have an impact. 'Skill' is not a checklist of things humans can do but an *integrated set of functionings* that are adjusted in response to the ongoing monitoring or 'sensing' of effects as the results of actions emerge. Here we return to the conundrum – what knowledge and skills do we as educators choose to help students develop? Perhaps the over-arching ability is that of developing new versions of these when they are needed, and combining and adapting existing knowledge and skills in order to improvise in new and unfamiliar situations.

The fourth component of capability that graduates should develop is *self-awareness*, the ability to recognise and evaluate the effects they are having and adjust what they are doing if necessary. Their preparedness and ability to reflect on a situation enables them to learn from their experience so that they can have more immediate effect and more impact in the future. Reflection is the key sense and meaning-making process in life; it ultimately feeds into what we value and our sense of fulfilment in life. The challenge for higher education is develop this ability in ways that are meaningful and relevant to students' lives and not simply an abstract exercise.

The successful application of capability in different situations produces effects (impact!) which nurture *confidence* and sustain willingness to try to achieve things that the individual or others value. But to turn ideas and feelings into action needs *opportunity* – to be provided with opportunity, to recognise and make good use of it, or be able to create one's own opportunities. So linked to opportunity is *freedom*

– without the freedom to choose and the freedom to create opportunities, the ability to achieve will be limited by the decisions of others. If we have freedom (autonomy) what is possible is only limited by our imagination, willingness and capability.

Vision for a graduate who can have impact on the world

For me, Richard Greene's (2004) detailed research-based account of the capabilities of high-performing people who have made a significant impact in their field provides an inspiring vision for the type of graduate we might aspire to develop.

> Highly effective people have eight general capabilities. The first four such capabilities are ways of using liberty they make for constructing, establishing, and founding enduring changes in lives and the world. They have ways, when encountering difference and otherness, of keeping what is new, difficult, and unknown or challenging from being absorbed and assimilated to their existing models and preferences. They have ways of preserving the otherness of what they encounter. Second, they have ways of unearthing the most buried, subtle, intimate, and vital forces and things inside themselves and examining them for possible use or improvement. Third, they have ways of bringing order to their own selves and to the selves of those in groups around them. Fourth, they have ways of turning insights, ideas, experiences, and the like into impacts on society, actual changes in how things are arranged and done. The second four general effectiveness capabilities are ways of protecting novelty from erosion by large, traditional, already established powers of the world. Fifth, they have ways of doing things with style and verve rather than doing them perfunctorily. Sixth, they have ways of upping the performance of all dimensions of their selves, work, and lives, not just some or a few. Seventh, they have ways of influencing people, in many channels, modes, and means. Eighth, and last, they have ways of operating with new common senses, they borrow or invent, that make their automatic reactions up-to-date and future-looking. (Greene, 2004: 5)

Greene's research focuses on exceptional people, high achievers in their field, and it might be argued that the capability constructs he has developed for exceptional people cannot be applied to individuals with more modest achievements. However, Greene's powerful way of framing the integrated capability and attitudes of people who are able to create an impact – *'they have ways of'* – points to the repertoire of strategies, skills, ways of thinking and being that people possess in order to achieve the things that they value in life. I believe that these repertoires can be nurtured and developed by taking a life-wide approach to education (Jackson in press) and by adopting many of the educational practices that are advocated in this book.

References

Greene, T. R. (2004) *32 Capabilities of Highly Effective People in Any Field*. Accessed 16/02/11 from at www.scribd.com/doc/2162334/32-Capabilities-of-Highly-Effective-Persons

Jackson, N. J. (ed) (in press) *Learning for a Complex World: A lifewide concept of learning, education and personal development*. (Authorhouse)

Rittel, H. and Webber, M. (1973) Dilemmas in a General Theory of Planning. *Policy Sciences* **4** 155–9

Sen, A. (1992) *Inequality Re-examined*. New York, Cambridge, MA: Russell Sage Foundation. Harvard University Press

NORMAN JACKSON is managing director of Chalk Mountain Education and Media Services and an emeritus professor of the University of Surrey. He was professor of higher education at Surrey and director of the Surrey Centre for Excellence in Professional Training and Education (SCEPTrE) whose primary focus was helping students develop their capabilities for the professional world.

He began his professional life as a geologist holding teaching, research and industrial posts in the UK and Saudi Arabia. A mid-career change via Her Majesty's Inspectorate, led him into higher education as a field of study and senior posts with the Higher Education Quality Council, Quality Assurance Agency, the Learning and Teaching Support Network (LTSN Generic Centre) and Higher Education Academy. Norman is no stranger to the challenge of trying to change the way people think out higher education. He has led a personal crusade to highlight the importance of students' creative development in higher education, and more recently developed the ideas of lifewide learning and education as a way of trying to encourage recognition of informal as well as formal learning gained during the higher education experience. You can find out more about Norman and his work at http://normanjackson.pbworks.com/

Graduate impact, student employability and academic integrity

Erica Morris
The Higher Education Academy

This chapter looks at the links between student employability and academic integrity. What critical strategies can be adopted to help students come to understand academic practice and develop the associated skills for information literacy, collaborative work and effective communication? How can we ensure that the skills for good academic practice are relevant and valued in other learning, community and working environments? Can we help to instil 'academic integrity' for graduates – and does this enhance graduate impact?

This chapter first examines student employability and how employers view those attributes and skills that relate to 'good academic practice', so we can explore the notion of academic integrity and its importance in higher education. This leads to the educational approaches and critical strategies that help students appreciate the importance of good academic practice and how these skills have an important part to play beyond their experiences at university or college.

Employability matters

Although there has been much discussion about the meaning of employability, it is helpful for the purposes of this chapter to have the following usable definition in mind:

> a set of achievements – skills, understandings and personal attributes – that make graduates more likely to gain employment and be successful in their chosen occupations, which benefits themselves, the workforce, the community and the economy.' (Yorke, 2006: 8)

In recent years, some work on student employability has focused on profiles to capture the knowledge and skills that students acquire through taking a particular subject or discipline in higher education. The profiles for business and management, hospitality, leisure and sport include skills that might be described as 'transferable' and relate to being an independent learner who can communicate effectively, work on their own initiative or collaboratively, and take responsibility for their own development (Rees et al, 2007). Indeed, these attributes and skills relate well to the 'generic' and 'personal' capabilities that employers value, including 'the ability to work with others in a team, communicate' and 'the ability and desire to learn for oneself and improve one's self-awareness and performance' (*ibid*: 4).

These observations are of course not ground-breaking, but the emphasis on transferable skills in employability profiles has had important implications for teaching, learning and assessment in higher education. There has been an increasing awareness that educators need to 'diversify' assessment, providing interesting and meaningful tasks that reflect the kinds of activities that students would engage with in the longer term and in the workplace, and that enable them to develop valuable transferable skills for team work and communicating, for example (Bloxham and Boyd, 2007).

But what attributes and skills do employers currently want from graduates? Jackson has provided a comprehensive analysis of the attributes and skills relevant to employers, highlighting a range of definitions and survey findings that shed light on their priority from industry or employer perspectives. This work also uncovers an important concern: a number of definitions have been used in empirical work and by stakeholders to describe particular competences or skills. This inconsistency in terminology, leading to an unclear research picture, could mean that higher education institutions (HEIs) focus on developing skills that are not seen as a priority by employers (Jackson, 2010). However, of particular interest here are those qualities and skills that are tied up with what is often termed 'good academic practice' in higher education, particularly personal or academic integrity, communication and working with others.

Drawing on established definitions and empirical work, Jackson's findings underline how 'ethics and responsibility', 'written communication' and 'team working' are deemed important competences by employers. For example, Jackson mentions findings indicating that honesty and integrity were seen as particularly important employability skills in UK graduates, with employers being generally satisfied with graduates' skills here (CIHE, 2008; IOD, 2007; cited in Jackson, 2010). There are, however, reported concerns with graduates' communication skills. In general, the analysis revealed that although written communication was seen as crucial, surveys indicated that employers tend to be dissatisfied with graduates' level of skill in this area (Jackson, 2010).

Jackson's work raises important issues about how we might effectively 'measure' student employability, and how stakeholders in industry, organisations and HEIs may well have differing understandings and views of particular skills and their relative importance. But of course, we need to 'bring in' the student here:

> To effectively enhance employability and the immediacy of adding value to enterprises, not only must businesses articulate what they need and want from graduates, it is also important that *graduates are aware of what they are learning and its use in the workplace*' (*ibid*: 55, my emphasis).

Academic integrity matters

Over the recent decade, in parallel with a growing emphasis on enhancing student employability in higher education, there has also been a focus on preventing and managing student plagiarism. This is not to say that there is direct linkage here. But it is interesting to find that in both these areas it is well-recognised that assessment, at the programme or course level, has a vital part to play in developing students' attributes and skills: it is through the use of authentic assessments that we can ensure that students can create original work and gain a range of transferable skills that are valued in varied contexts, including the workplace.

A number of pertinent issues concerning student plagiarism have been considered in the literature, including, for example: whether there has been an increase in cases of student plagiarism in higher education, identifying the likely reasons for unacceptable academic practice, and how educational approaches and tools can be used to prevent inadvertent plagiarism (Power, 2009; Selwyn, 2008; Walker, 2009). Interestingly, in the debate around student plagiarism over the last decade there has been a move towards recognising that HEIs need to promote 'academic integrity' [1] as part of an institutional approach developed to address plagiarism through educational measures and robust regulations (MacDonald and Carroll, 2006; Park, 2004). In outlining a framework for addressing student plagiarism, Park has stressed how it must be informed by a number of 'core pillars' including one of 'academic integrity':

> The academic enterprise is rooted in a culture of integrity, founded on honesty and mutual trust ... Academic integrity should be valued and promoted by the institution and it should underpin ... all aspects of its teaching and learning strategy (2004; 297–98).

But how might such values as honesty be instilled in students? Clearly, teaching, learning and assessment strategies have an important part to play, as do regulations or codes of conduct, to which students are typically introduced through university induction programmes. However, empirical work has indicated that although students may well be aware of university policy covering unacceptable academic practice, they do not necessarily read it or know what it covers (Power, 2009; Ryan et al, 2009). These findings suggest that it is insufficient to assume that providing coherent policy and procedures to students will make a difference to their understandings about academic practice and the associated behaviours and skills.

As Ryan and associates note, students do not necessarily relate policy to their own study and the strategies that they may use to produce assignments. Innovative approaches to assessment can help students learn about good academic practice, but complementary 'tactics' are also needed to engage students in discussions about academic honesty and established practice. An additional challenge is how we might

---

1   As a notion, 'academic integrity' has been defined as an adherence to these values: 'honesty, trust, fairness, respect, and responsibility' (The Center for Academic Integrity, 1999: 4).

enable students to see the links between academic integrity in an educational environment and personal integrity in the workplace.

Clarkeburn and Freeman (2007) have described an institutional strategy designed to promote 'academic honesty', which has involved a range of approaches including, for example: business students taking an online module covering academic honesty, staff development opportunities on assessment design, and teaching sessions involving staff–student dialogue about academic honesty. Importantly, the focus here has been on encouraging good academic practice:

> this is in line with the tertiary educational process, developing students to graduate as ethical self-regulating professionals. External rules-based strategies addressing motivations to be dishonest are inadequate in achieving this on their own (*ibid*: 22).

It is widely recognised that students currently entering higher education bring with them a wide range of experiences and skills, and students need opportunities through orientation and induction programmes at the subject level to gain skills for higher education study, particularly those required for researching and presenting information, and academic writing (including citation and referencing). Over recent years, there has also been an emphasis on assessments involving group work to help students gain skills in working collaboratively. In this area, students must be given opportunities to understand the nature of collaborative working, as there can be confusion leading to (unintentional) student collusion (The Academy JISC Academic Integrity Service, 2010). Indeed, it has been suggested that with an educational focus on group and team working, this may have contributed to possible increases in cases of collusion (Ryan et al, 2009).

Developing students: critical strategies and issues

Higher education can not only help to foster the development of attributes and skills that are important for employability, but can also enable students to develop an understanding of good academic practice and associated values. It is vital that programmes in HEIs provide opportunities for students to learn and rehearse the competences for personal or academic integrity, information literacy, communication and collaborative work. It is also clear that educational approaches must be designed to support students' personal development planning and the development of critical thinking skills, so that they can readily assess their own learning and progress (for example, Buswell and Tomkins, 2008). The following areas relate to what can be termed critical strategies that can be employed to promote the development of students' skills relevant to both student employability and academic integrity.

Student mentoring

Peer mentoring or e-mentoring has been used to support students' transition to higher education (Hill and Reddy, 2007; Hixenbaugh et al, 2005). It is also an approach that might be beneficial in helping new students come to understand and take on the values and behaviours associated with personal and academic integrity. Indeed, as part of their multi-faceted strategy to promote academic honesty within an institution, Clarkeburn and Freeman (2007) have reported that peer mentoring has become an important way to bridge new students' experiences of university, along with induction events and activities that involve the 'student voice' in encouraging good academic practice.

Assessment design

Approaches to assessment can have important implications for whether students have opportunities to acquire an understanding of, and the necessary skills for, good academic practice and accordingly, whether the possibilities for inadvertent plagiarism are minimised. For example, good practice guidance has described how educators can 'design out' plagiarism through re-thinking assessments for students (Carroll, 2007; Plagiarismadvice, 2009). But interestingly, it is not the 'designing-out' that really matters: if there is a focus on devising authentic assessment tasks that are original, meaningful and interesting then students are likely to engage in the learning process and develop usable skills that will serve them well in all sorts of contexts.

For example, Graham (n.d) has outlined the use of real or live projects involving students taking hospitality, tourism, and festival and event management who work in a group acting as consultants for an external organisation. Here, groups of students carry out particular projects provided by an organisation, who meet them on a regular basis. The client organisation also gives feedback on the project work and students' team working, as well as contributing to the marks for the reports. With support from the tutor and organisation, student teams develop a methodology, study the presenting issue, and provide an oral and written report. Graham notes how this kind of assessment helps students to acquire skills and qualities, such as those for team working, professional behaviour, communication and time management.

McGowan and Lightbody have stressed the importance of re-visiting the matter of plagiarism and referencing throughout a programme of study. In the context of a financial-accounting course, these researchers have described the use of a particularly inspired assignment to educate students about plagiarism. Students completed an online workshop covering plagiarism and referencing, and were then to read a prepared 'plagiarised' essay on an area of accounting and the associated information sources, and to appropriately include the citations. This prepared essay included a number of different forms of plagiarism (for example, changed quotations). The students were also required to build on the essay by writing a conclusion for the topic. Findings indicated that this assignment helped students gain an understanding of plagiarism and referencing and, importantly, there were no cases of plagiarised material identified in the students' written conclusions or on a following course assignment (McGowan and Lightbody, 2008).

Web technologies and tools

In recent years, there has been a move towards using web technologies and tools, such as blogs and wikis, for the purposes of assessment. These can be used effectively for collaborative learning and to support the development of transferable skills (Minocha, 2009). However, a recent project has looked at the possibilities and challenges for assessment and academic integrity when web tools for authoring and collaboration are used. Lecturers reported issues related to how students' work could be openly viewed by other students, such as on a wiki. For example, students might be concerned about publishing their work online, thinking that other students might copy it. Issues relating to supporting students in employing different styles of writing for online authoring were also apparent, as were challenges faced in assessing and marking student contributions in a web 2.0 environment (Waycott et al, 2010). In the areas of business, management, hospitality, leisure, sport and tourism education, it would be valuable to look at the implications of using web tools for assessment, academic integrity and the development of transferable skills.

Conclusion

So, we find that innovative and authentic approaches to assessment are important in higher education because they not only mean that students can engage with producing original work, but because they can be employed to encourage students to develop the transferable skills that employers value highly.

It would be fruitful to further explore the important links between student employability and academic integrity by undertaking empirical work of a longitudinal nature. This could investigate how personal and academic integrity, and the skills associated with good academic practice are viewed and valued by organisations – helping to assess the impact of current graduates. This work could also explore the views of recent graduates on the relevance of these values and skills to employment. It is recognised that organisations or employers need to work in partnership with HEIs to clarify the required graduate skills (Maxwell et al, 2010). As Graham (n.d) aptly pointed out in highlighting the use of live projects as a form of assessment: 'The university benefits include building links and networks in the wider business community and a better understanding of employers' requirements with respect to graduate skills'.

References

Bloxham, S. and Boyd, P. (2007) *Developing Effective Assessment in Higher Education: a practical guide.* Maidenhead, UK: Open University Press, McGraw-Hill Education

Buswell, J. and Tomkins, A. (2008) Enhancing employability through critical reflective learning. In S. Graves and A. Maher (2008) *Developing Graduate Employability. Case Studies in Hospitality, Leisure, Sport and Tourism.* Newbury, Berks: Threshold Press

Carroll, J. (2007) *A Handbook for Deterring Plagiarism in Higher Education.* 2nd ed. Oxford: Oxford Centre for Staff and Learning Development, Oxford Brookes University

Clarkeburn, H. and Freeman, M. (2007) To plagiarise or not to plagiarise: an online approach to improving and motivating honest academic writing. *International Journal of Management Education* 6 (3) 21–33

Council for Industry and Higher Education (2008) *Graduate employability: What do employers think and want?* Cited in Jackson (2010)

Graham, J. (n.d) *Live Projects*. Employability case study. Accessed 18 January 2011 from: http://www.heacademy.ac.uk/hlst/resources/casestudies/

Hill, R. and Reddy, P. (2007) Undergraduate peer mentoring: an investigation into processes, activities and outcomes. *Psychology Learning and Teaching* 6 (2) 98–103. Accessed 18 January 2011 from: http://www.wwwords.co.uk/

Hixenbaugh, P., Dewart, H., Drees, D. and Williams, D. (2005) Peer e-mentoring: enhancement of the first year experience. *Psychology Learning and Teaching* 5 (1) 8–14. Accessed 18 January 2011 from: http://www.wwwords.co.uk/

Institute of Directors (2007) *Graduates employability skills*. Institute of Directors skills briefing, December 2007: Cited in Jackson (2010)

Jackson, D. (2010) An international profile of industry-relevant competencies and skill gaps in modern graduates. *International Journal of Management Education* 8 (3) 29–58

MacDonald, R. and Carroll, J. (2006) Plagiarism – a complex issue requiring a holistic institutional approach. *Assessment and Evaluation in Higher Education* 31 (2) 233–45

McGowan, S. and Lightbody, M. (2008) 'Another chance to practice': Repeating plagiarism education for EAL students within a discipline context. *International Journal for Educational Integrity* 4 (1) 16–30. Accessed 18 January 2010 from: http://www.ojs.unisa.edu.au/

Maxwell, G., Scott, B., Macfarlane, D. and Williamson, E. (2010) Employers as stakeholders in postgraduate employability skills development. *International Journal of Management Education* 8 (2) 1-11

Minocha, S. (2009) A Study on the Effective Use of Social Software by Further and Higher Education in the UK to Support Student Learning and Engagement (Final Report). Accessed 9 November 2009 from: http://www.jisc.ac.uk/whatwedo/projects/

Park, C. (2004) Rebels without a clause: towards an institutional framework for dealing with plagiarism by students. *Journal of Further and Higher Education* 28 (3) 291–306

Plagiarismadvice.org (2009) *Developing assessment strategies which encourage original student work: an online guide*. Accessed 8 October 2009 from: http://www.plagiarismadvice.org/

Power, L. G. (2009) University Students' Perceptions of Plagiarism. *The Journal of Higher Education* 80 (6) 643–62

Rees, C., Forbes, P. and Kubler, B. (2007) *Student employability profiles: A guide for higher education practitioners*. Graduate Prospects, The Council for Industry and Higher Education, The Higher Education Academy. Accessed 4 October 2010 from: http://www.heacademy.ac.uk/

Ryan, G., Bonanno, H., Krass, I., Scouller, K. and Smith, L. (2009) Undergraduate and Postgraduate Pharmacy Students Perceptions of Plagiarism and Academic Honesty. *American Journal of Pharmaceutical Education* 73 (6) 1–8

Selwyn, N. (2008) 'Not necessarily a bad thing...': a study of online plagiarism amongst undergraduate students. *Assessment & Evaluation in Higher Education* 33 (5) 465–79

The Academy JISC Academic Integrity Service (2010) *Supporting academic integrity: approaches and resources for higher education*. The Higher Education Academy. Accessed 18 January 2011 from: http://www.heacademy.ac.uk/

The Center for Academic Integrity (1999) *The Fundamental Values of Academic Integrity*. Des Plaines, IL: Office of College Relations at Oakton Community College. Accessed 23 August 2010 from: http://www.academicintegrity.org/

Walker, J. (2009) Measuring plagiarism: researching what students do, not what they say they do. *Studies in Higher Education* 35 (1) 41–59

Waycott, J., Gray, K., Clerehan, R., Hamilton, M., Richardson, J., Sheard, J. and Thompson, C. (2010) Implications for academic integrity of using web 2.0 for teaching, learning and assessment in higher education. *International Journal for Educational Integrity* 6 (2) 8–18. Accessed 18 January 2011 from: http://www.ojs.unisa.edu.au/

Yorke, M. (2006) *Employability in higher education: what it is – what it is not.* Learning and Employability Series 1. ESEC Team, The Higher Education Academy. Accessed 17 January 2011 from: http://www.heacademy.ac.uk/

ERICA MORRIS is a senior adviser for quality enhancement and assessment at the Higher Education Academy with a particular interest in academic integrity and student plagiarism. She has worked in the higher education sector for 17 years on teaching and learning initiatives, research in learning technologies and in educational support, and has published papers in the areas of student learning, statistical education and educational technology. Previously at the Open University, Erica has worked in the areas of learning skills, instructional design, careers education, personal development planning and e-portfolios.

2

Engaging students, staff and employers in enhancing graduate impact
Tourism Management at the University of Gondar

Mark Goodwin[1], Gojjam Ademe[2], Martin Pennington[3]
Craig Bartle[1] and Paul Jackson[3]
University of Leicester and University of Gondar

This chapter describes a collaborative project to measure and develop the impact of graduates from the BA in Tourism Management programme at the University of Gondar in the north-western highlands of Ethiopia. The approach used intentions surveys, destinations data and an employability audit involving students, staff and employers to develop the curriculum, promote employer engagement and develop transition support that will bridge the gap between undergraduate programmes and further education or graduate-level employment.

Introduction

Ethiopia is a country facing a number of daunting social and economic challenges. It is also a country with a resourceful and resilient people who are proud of their history and culture – and keen to share it with others. Ethiopia's economy is growing faster than most in Africa, and drafts of the Government's latest five-year Growth and Transformation Plan (GAP) aim to help the country to move from a strategy dependent on foreign investment to one driven by developments within the country – including education and tourism (MoFED, 2010).

Ethiopia has already taken impressive steps to improve its education system at all levels. It is one of the few African states likely to meet the United Nations' Millennium Development Goal (MDG) of providing universal access to primary education, and there are no fees for primary or secondary state education. A little over a decade ago the country had two public universities and higher education (HE) was reserved for a privileged elite. Now there are 22 public universities with another ten at the planning stage. The number of students in each institution has, on average, almost doubled over the past few years and is expected to double again in the near future.

---

1   GENIE Centre for Excellence in Teaching and Learning, Department of Genetics, University of Leicester

2   Department of Tourism Management, University of Gondar; now Department of Management, Debre Markos University

3   Student Support and Development Service, University of Leicester

This rapid growth has not been without its challenges, however, and concerns have been expressed that the curricula, teaching methods and assessment strategies are struggling to produce a new generation of graduates who will be able to have an effective impact on the country's future.

An attractive destination for ambitious graduates is Ethiopia's growing tourism sector. The potential is enormous: Ethiopia contains eight UNESCO World Heritage sites, as many as Egypt, and more than most other countries in Africa. But exploiting this potential depends on a supply of graduates with the right combination of knowledge and skills to be able to make a difference in an increasingly competitive global environment. Ethiopia remains a popular destination for the adventurous traveller, but broadening its appeal depends on improving the infrastructure and developing a generation of managers and innovators with the right combination of attitudes, knowledge and skills.

The Department of Tourism Management at the University of Gondar was the first of its kind in eastern Africa, and it aims to produce graduates with impact through its BA in Tourism Management programme. The programme has a detailed and comprehensive curriculum, but developing the programme – and transition support to assist the students in moving from study to work – has been hampered by a lack of information about the destinations of graduates. There has also been little information so far about graduate impact, about the extent to which the programme's content and delivery have been effective in producing graduates able to find employment at the right sort of level to enable them to instigate change.

The project described in this chapter was designed to improve the impact of graduates from the BA in Tourism Management programme, and formed part of a long-standing

Figure 2.1
The Simien
Mountains,
some 130 km
to the north-
east of Gondar.
(*Elizabeth Draper*)

link between the University of Leicester and the University of Gondar. Gondar was founded in 1636 by the Emperor Fasilides and was the capital of Ethiopia for some 200 years. It is situated in the north-western highlands of Ethiopia, in the foothills of the Simien Mountains, some 500 km from the modern capital of Addis Ababa. The town is popular with tourists, and is dominated by six castle-like palaces and a number of other buildings that make up the Royal Enclosure (see Plates 1 and 2).

The link between the Universities of Leicester and Gondar dates back to the establishment of the University of Gondar in 2004, although there had already been links between health professionals in Leicester and the Gondar College of Medical Sciences (the university's precursor). By 2010, Gondar University had expanded from a training college to a multidisciplinary higher-education institution (HEI) with seven faculties and some 10,000 full-time undergraduate and postgraduate students. The intention is to expand to some 25,000 full-time students over the next ten years.

In 2008 a member of the UK project team – Mark Goodwin – visited Gondar to discuss arrangements for a collaborative Leicester–Gondar PhD programme to develop research capacity. During his stay he met Gojjam Ademe, the head of the Department of Tourism Management, and discussed some of the problems associated with developing graduate impact in the UK and Ethiopia. Later, he was invited to attend a coffee ceremony at the home of a recent graduate from the BA in Tourism Management programme. The student lived on the edge of Gondar in a one-room dwelling with his mother, his sister and his sister's child. He was looking for work, full of enthusiasm for the potential of Ethiopian tourism, and keen to apply the knowledge he had gained to develop a career. What was less clear was how he could find a suitable position, or to what extent his peers were successful in finding graduate-level employment.

These meetings, and a well-timed funding call from the Education Partnerships in Africa (EPA) programme (British Council, 2011), managed by the British Council and funded by the UK Department of Business, Innovation and Skills (BIS), led to the development of a joint proposal for a project to measure and develop the impact of graduates. The approach would be trialled using a cohort from Gondar's BA in Tourism Management programme, but it was clear that the methodology – and the lessons learned – could have a much wider application.

The core project team comprised Mark Goodwin and Craig Bartle of the GENIE Centre for Excellence in Teaching and Learning (CETL) at the University of Leicester, Gojjam Ademe of the Department of Tourism Management at the University of Gondar, and Martin Pennington and Paul Jackson of the Student Support and Development Service at the University of Leicester.

Description

From the outset, it was clear that we needed to undertake a number of separate – but linked – projects.

Initially, we needed to find out something about the career intentions of the cohort before graduation, and link this to information about their destinations after graduation. It is difficult to develop impact before you've started to measure it, and some indication of the students' roles after graduation would inform us about their ability to make a difference. But destinations must be interpreted in the light of aspirations (in the UK as much as in Ethiopia): true impact – true success – lies in a graduate's ability to obtain work or further education that reflects their long-term career goals.

Then we needed to look at what the students, teaching staff and future employers thought made the most important contribution to graduate impact, as well as their perceptions of how well those elements were delivered in the BA in Tourism Management and the transition support available. To develop the programme to ensure that it produced graduates with the qualities necessary to have an impact, we had to examine what the students and teachers thought those qualities were, and then compare their perceptions with those of employers.

Lastly, we wanted to use the whole process to develop the working relationship between employers and the students and staff in the Department of Tourism Management. All three share a common goal: the development of graduates with impact. A concern – in both the UK and Ethiopia – is a perceived lack of engagement between HEIs and employers: the notion that HEIs and their programmes are somehow 'out of touch' with the real world. The expansion of HE in Ethiopia has resulted in the development of a range of vocational courses designed to produce graduates with impact for specific sectors. The challenge is to ensure that the knowledge and skills provided are in line with the employment needs of new graduates and their employers.

Methodology

The methodology involved a two-pronged approach.

First, matched questionnaires were used to link information about the cohort's intentions before graduation with their destinations some six months later. The Student–Intentions questionnaire was given to the undergraduates at the end of their degree programme and asked about career aspirations, as well as recording details of any employment, further education or training already arranged. It also provided essential contact information for the subsequent Student–Destinations questionnaire, which asked about their employment or education arrangements some six months after graduation. Both questionnaires were based, with permission, on the Destinations of Leavers from Higher Education questionnaire produced by the UK Higher Education Statistics Agency Limited (2010).

Second, this data was combined with matched reports on aspects of employability from staff, students and employers. The Student–Employability and Staff–Employability questionnaires asked students and teaching staff about their perceptions of the importance of specific aspects of graduate impact and the extent to which they were covered by the current BA in Tourism Management programme (using a 0–4 Likert scale). Both questionnaires were developed, with permission, from the UK Centre for Biosciences' (2008) Employability Audit survey.

The Employer–Employability questionnaire used a similar approach to look at employers' awareness of the programme; their willingness to become involved in its development (for example, by providing work placements or visiting the university) and their perceptions of the skills and characteristics required for graduate impact. It was developed by the project team. (The employers were identified from information in the Student–Intentions and Student–Destinations questionnaires.)

The data gathering phase was followed by two workshops. The first, held in the UK, allowed the project team to analyse the results, identify priority areas, and discuss possible interventions to develop graduate impact. The second, held in Gondar, brought together existing students, recent graduates, teaching staff and a selection of employers to discuss the implications of the project outcomes (and improved employer engagement). In the event, this second workshop also included members of the management team at the University of Gondar, teaching staff from other Ethiopian HEIs and representatives from the Ministry of Culture and Tourism.

The intention was to produce an analysis that could develop graduate impact through changes to the curriculum, improved links with employers, and better systems to monitor and improve the transition from study to work.

The programme was as follows (dates are included to give some indication of the timescales):

Destination questionnaires

Student–Intentions	End of degree programme (June 2009)
Student–Destinations	Six months after graduation (January 2010)

Employability questionnaires

Student–Employability	End of degree programme (June 2009)
Staff–Employability	End of degree programme (June 2009)
Employer–Employability	End of degree programme onwards (June 2009 ▷)

▽

UK Workshop (March 2010): project team and others
❑ analysis
❑ priorities and possible interventions

▽

Ethiopia Workshop (April 2010): project team plus undergraduates, graduates, teaching staff, employers, representatives of the Ministry of Culture and Tourism and others (see figure 2)
❑ graduate impact: curriculum development / systems to support transition
❑ employer engagement

Outcomes

There is not room here for a detailed discussion of the results, but a few points will demonstrate how an approach of this sort can help to evaluate – as well as develop – graduate impact.

The destination questionnaires indicated that most of the graduates had found a job six months after graduation (an impressive 72%), and most were working in roles associated with tourism (95% of those employed). However, over half reported that they were still actively looking for work even though they had jobs (57%) – and few had been successful in finding places in further education (2%), despite the fact that almost half were looking (47%). A plausible interpretation is that the new graduates were able to find jobs, but not necessarily jobs that matched their initial expectations as in terms of impact.

This picture of an ambitious – and mobile – cohort is supported by the fact that only a third (35%) claimed that they had accepted their current position because 'it fitted into my career plan/was exactly the work I wanted'. This interpretation, if correct, indicates some obvious limitations with respect to graduates' impact at the start of their careers, and may go some way to explain the demand for further – postgraduate – education and training.

The ambition of the graduates to make an impact was apparent in the employability questionnaires. Before graduation, the students wanted more information about potential career paths and the destinations of past graduates. The emphasis was on developing careers rather than obtaining employment *per se*. They wanted to establish links with employers before graduation, and were aware of the need to leave with evidence that they possessed specific key skills (for example, formal assessment of their ability to work in other languages). Interestingly, the students were more confident than the staff that they understood the skills that would be necessary to have an impact over the next few years.

For their part, the employers were just as keen to make contact with the students and the Department of Tourism Management. Some three-quarters (75%) expressed an interest in developing a link, and almost all were happy to volunteer for specific forms of engagement: for example, to advise on – or even deliver – aspects of the curriculum related to the working environment; to provide work placements; or to engage in collaborative research on graduate impact. Again, there is a danger of over-interpreting the results, but the employers seemed to recognise that their own success depended on a supply of graduates with the characteristics necessary to have a real impact in a growing and changing work environment – a perception supported by the fact that the attributes they valued most were 'problem-solving skills' (76%) and 'leadership' (84%).

Evaluation

A project has to be evaluated in terms of its aims and objectives. With this project we hoped to develop a general methodology to develop graduate impact, one that could be applied to other programmes in Ethiopia, the UK and elsewhere. In trialling the approach with the BA in Tourism Management at Gondar we had a number of specific objectives:

- ❑ An analysis of student intentions, graduate destinations and the transition process.
- ❑ A robust methodology to support continued monitoring of graduate intentions and destinations.
- ❑ Established links with employers based on a documented willingness to engage in curriculum development and delivery.
- ❑ The engagement of students, staff and employers in structured discussions about the development of graduate impact.
- ❑ Specific changes to the curriculum and its delivery to promote graduate impact.
- ❑ Specific systems and resources to support transition.

It is safe to say that the project met its objectives, although a number of the outcomes – for example, changes to the curriculum – are still at the development stage.

The Gondar trial also had a number of unexpected, though very welcome, outcomes that resulted from the Ethiopia Workshop, which brought together past and present students, teaching staff from a number of HEIs, employers and the Ministry of Culture and Tourism.

- ❑ An agreement to work towards the development of a national employability centre for the Ethiopian HE sector.
- ❑ An agreement to work towards the establishment of a national association of

Figure 2.2
The Ethiopia
Workshop at the
University of Gondar,
with Gojjam Ademe,
Martin Pennington,
Craig Bartle and Mark
Goodwin (from left).
(*Mark Goodwin*)

tourism professionals.

Both of these initiatives have clear implications for the development of graduate impact in the future by addressing some of the issues identified in the project. The employability centre will allow the sector to share resources and expertise in terms of embedding notions of graduate impact into curricula and transition support. The association of tourism professionals will provide a forum to continue the discussions started at the Ethiopia workshop: to make the development of graduate impact something that is the responsibility of students (before and after graduation), teaching staff and university management, employers and those charged with the development of the sector (in this case, the Ministry of Culture and Tourism).

Discussion

This one-year project aimed to improve graduate impact for a single programme at a single Ethiopian HEI, but it has obvious implications for improving the impact of graduates from other Ethiopian HEIs (and HEIs further afield). The results also have implications for the UK: first, because many of the issues are similar, and second because we think the methodology used here can be adapted to develop graduate impact in UK HEIs. Indeed, the approach is currently being used as part of a project funded by the UK Centre for Bioscience to develop graduate impact in biosciences students at the University of Leicester.

Graduate impact is clearly related to student destinations: specifically, to graduates' ability to obtain and retain graduate-level employment and be successful in managing a career in the longer term (which is closely linked to notions of 'employability'). However, our findings suggest that the interpretation of destinations data depends on an understanding of students' aspirations and intentions (in the UK as much as in Ethiopia). Knowing something about students' employment or study some six months after graduation is made far more meaningful if it is placed in the context of their intentions before graduation (and, perhaps, of their intentions before entering higher education). A graduate working in a bookshop is fine if that graduate's long-term plans included a career in the management of the book business; it is less satisfactory if he or she had always wanted a career in academic research.

Graduates' ability to have an impact in the career that they aspire to is linked to the attributes of the graduates themselves, as well as to perceptions of the strengths and weaknesses of their previous educational experiences. This is crucial to the students' ability to negotiate the transition from study to work, and to demonstrate to employers that they have the transferable skills necessary to succeed in a graduate-level position (assuming that sufficient positions are available).

Our work in Gondar indicated that one of the main limitations in terms of graduate impact is the ability to secure graduate-level employment. This seems to be recognised by all the parties involved, and all agreed that addressing the problem required them to work together to ensure that the process does not begin and end with the content and delivery of undergraduate programmes. This involves more than 'employer engagement'. Students, HEI staff, employers and the Ministry of Culture and Tourism need to work together to establish systems that will allow the students to move from study to work in a way that recognises the skills that they have acquired as 'graduates', as well as the contribution that these skills will allow them to make. Employers certainly need to engage with the HEI's staff and students, but it was clear that the reverse is also true.

The UK context – with its larger and more mature tourism sector – provides a useful comparison here. The issue of developing graduate impact in the UK is more clearly defined, monitored and recognised, although there are still problems in securing graduate-level employment, particularly in the current recession, and there are perennial reports of skills deficits from employers. In the UK, a total of 117 FE and HE institutions offered undergraduate courses in tourism in 2009 (Thomas, 2007; Walmsley, 2009). Of the UK/EU graduates completing courses in 2007–08, about 50% were in full-time paid work six months after graduation, about 15% opted for further study and about 9% were assumed to be unemployed. Roughly 50% of those in full-time employment were in graduate-level jobs. (Graduates were more likely to be in a graduate job if they were in a medium-sized firm; those in larger firms were less likely to be in a graduate job.)

In the UK, as in Ethiopia, graduate impact is clearly seen as important, although there is some concern that tourism has not been professionalised as effectively as other occupations. The UK Institute of Travel and Tourism (ITT) appears to be taking a lead in increasing the level of professionalism and is working closely with universities to develop the sector – and there would seem to be a similar role here for the proposed association of tourism professionals in Ethiopia. In this respect, a simple survey of destinations after six months is not enough: HEIs must work with employers (and those, such as the ministry in Ethiopia, that regulate the employment market) to take into account students' career intentions, to help them to match these against the opportunities that are available, and to provide them with the evidence necessary to be successful in an increasingly competitive – and globalised – employment market.

The days when it was enough for HEIs to 'wave goodbye at the door' to graduating students are long past. Employers must engage with HEIs, and HEIs must engage with the workplace, to monitor, develop and evaluate graduate impact. Important elements include

❏ monitoring the transition of students from undergraduate programmes to further study or employment (and beyond)
❏ developing systems to support transition that bridge study and work, and to ensure that those systems are coherent
❏ initiating an effective working relationship between HEIs, employers and those responsible for public policy with respect to graduate impact.

In this respect, an intentions–destinations survey combined with an employability audit acts as both an evaluation of the effectiveness of the transition process and an indication as to how it might be improved. As Nigussie Mitiku, the director of institutional quality assurance at Debre Markos University, in describing the impact of this project, put it:

> Higher education institutions in Ethiopia need to embed employability skills in their curriculum to ensure quality education and produce successful graduates. The in-depth investigation you made in this regard could be a model for higher institutions in Ethiopia.

In closing, the graduate from the BA in Tourism Management programme mentioned in the introduction has now found employment: he is working as an official guide to the Royal Enclosure Complex in Gondar (see Plate 1). He is using his deep knowledge of the site, and his excellent spoken English, to introduce visitors to one of the wonders of Ethiopian culture. In time, he hopes to progress to have an even more significant impact on the development of Ethiopian tourism.

Main learning points

❑ Collaborative projects of this sort work best when they are true partnerships, involving a sharing of expertise and experiences, with clear and explicit benefits for both sides.

❑ Data on graduate destinations must be interpreted in the light of information about students' aspirations and intentions before they leave their undergraduate programmes.

❑ Graduate impact depends on graduates' ability to find graduate-level employment and/or further education and training. This, in turn, depends on the perceptions of students, teaching staff and employers about the knowledge and skills the graduates have acquired in the course of their undergraduate programmes.

❑ Developing graduate impact requires a discussion involving teachers in HEIs, employers and the students themselves to develop appropriate curricula and transition systems that can bridge the gap between study and work to allow new graduates to identify suitable opportunities and provide evidence that they have the attributes necessary to succeed in graduate-level roles.

❑ A simple questionnaire-based methodology – linking data about intentions and destinations to the perceptions of students, staff and employers – can provide a transferable way of initiating those discussions and promoting employer engagement.

References and URLs

British Council (2011) *Education Partnerships in Africa (EPA)*. Accessed 5 January 2011 from http://www.britishcouncil.org/learning-epa-about.htm

Higher Education Statistics Agency Limited (2010) *Destinations of Leavers from Higher Education 2008/09* (January 2010). Accessed 5 January 2011 from http://www.hesa.ac.uk/index.php

MoFED (Ministry of Finance and Economic Development) (2010) *Growth and Transformation Plan* (GTP) 2010/11–2014/15 (draft). Addis Ababa, MoFED

Thomas, R. (2007) *Professionalism in Travel and Tourism*, Leeds, Institute of Travel and Tourism. Accessed 5 January 2011 from http://www.itt.co.uk/documents/itt_research_report_2007

UK Centre for Bioscience (2008) *Employability Audit*. Accessed 5 January 2011 from http://www.bioscience.heacademy.ac.uk/ftp/employability/empaudit.pdf

Walmsley, A. (2009) *ATHE Report on Tourism Higher Education in the UK*. Brighton: Association for Tourism in Higher Education. Accessed 5 January 2011 from http://www.athe.org.uk/publications/TIM2009Final_April_2010.pdf

MARK GOODWIN is a teaching fellow in the GENIE Centre for Excellence in Teaching and Learning (CETL), which is based in the Department of Genetics at the University of Leicester. He has also worked for the UK government's Overseas Development Administration and The Open University. His interests include open educational resources (OERs), the links between education and development, aspects of graduate employability, and the teaching of bioethics and sustainable development. He manages the Leicester–Gondar PhD programme, and is involved with a number of other projects as part of the link between the Universities of Leicester and Gondar. For further information please contact Dr Mark Goodwin, GENIE, Department of Genetics, University of Leicester, University Road, Leicester LE1 7RH, UK. Email: majg1@le.ac.uk. Telephone: +44 (0)116 225 3489.

GOJJAM ADEME is currently head of the Department of Management at Debre Markos University, which is about 300 kilometres to the north-west of Addis Ababa. He is also a member of the university's strategic planning committee. Before moving to Debre Markos he worked for the University of Gondar for eight years as a lecturer and head of department in the Department of Business Management and Tourism Management.

MARTIN PENNINGTON is a member of the University of Leicester's Student Support and Development Service (SSDS). His work involves policy development, quality assurance, service evaluation, and project management. His professional background is in careers, initially in schools and colleges and subsequently at the University of Leicester where he was Careers Service Head for eight years. During this period he collaborated with colleagues in Israel, Finland and the USA. He is a board director for the Association of Graduate Careers Advisory Services (AGCAS), and is currently investigating student retention and student success at the University of Leicester.

CRAIG BARTLE is a research assistant in the GENIE CETL in the Department of Genetics at the University of Leicester. He has an MSc in social research methods, and has worked on social research projects at the University of Northumbria, the University of Sheffield and the University of Nottingham. Craig is currently investigating student retention and student success at the University of Leicester.

PAUL JACKSON is director of the Student Support and Development Service at the University of Leicester, and provides strategic leadership for student development (careers, study and research skills), counselling, welfare, AccessAbility (disability services), mental well-being and Student Healthy Living services. He is responsible for the university's employability strategy, PDP development, work-related learning and other initiatives that support the student experience. Recent developments include an internal and external graduate internship scheme; a graduate business start-up scheme; a university jobshop; and a counselling research centre. External recognition includes a *THES* Award for Outstanding Support for Students for the AccessAbility project 2009/2010.

ACKNOWLEDGEMENTS

The authors would like to thank the British Council in the UK and Ethiopia for their assistance through the Education Partnerships in Africa (EPA) programme, and the UK Department of Business, Innovation and Skills (BIS) for funding the project. We would also like to thank Dr Mengesha Admassu, the president of the University of Gondar, and Dr Desalegn Mengesha, the vice-president for academic, research and community services, for their assistance, as well as Professor Mike Silverman, Nichole Bruce and Solomon Assefa of the Leicester–Gondar Link, and Professor Annette Cashmore, the Director of the GENIE Centre for Excellence in Teaching and Learning (CETL). Finally, thanks are due to Kirsty Lawrence for her assistance with background research into tourism and higher education in Ethiopia.

This document is an output from the EPA Project funded by the UK Department of Business, Innovation and Skills (BIS) for the benefit of the African further and higher education sector and the UK higher education Sector; The views expressed are not necessarily those of BIS or the British Council.

3

Profiling the international postgraduate student experience

Julia Pointon
De Montfort University

This research with international postgraduate students over a five-year period sought to understand the rich tapestry created by international students, looking at experience before arrival, their experience of study in the UK, their experience on return to their home country and finally, the experience of employers from overseas who recruit UK graduates to make an impact. It highlights how staff can manage differing previous student pedagogic experiences and practices that necessarily shape the way non-UK students engage with the conventions of UK education.

Background

De Montfort University (DMU Leicester) has witnessed an unprecedented growth in the total number of non-UK full-time students at both undergraduate and masters level. In September 2010 the business school alone had 618 international students, and the range of countries represented is also increasing. At DMU in September 2010 over 80 different countries were represented and we are not exceptional. The total number of non UK students in the UK has continued to rise from 325,985 in 2007–08 to 368,970 in 2008–9, an increase of 8%. The strongest growth was in full-time taught postgraduate programmes (up 17% for non-UK students), followed by full-time undergraduate study (up 8%). The total economic value generated by non-UK students is in excess of £3.26 billion (UUK, 2009).

Non-UK students represent an important economic consideration and potential income stream for many universities, but to assume this will remain the case for the foreseeable future would be naive in the extreme. In Australia, for example, the bubble burst in 2008 and 2009, triggered in part by attacks on Indian students, and by investigations into shady private colleges that offered to help people emigrate and become permanent residents. The number of foreign students in the country began to decline rapidly. The Australian response has been a reorientation of regulations designed to make it easier to remain in the country after graduation. The US, also witnessing a decline in total international students, has set up a review designed to strengthen safety and openness in an attempt to win back some of the market sector. India has set its sights on becoming recognised as one of the top educational

21

destinations (University World News, 2011), and is planning to develop fourteen 'innovation universities' which will focus on various research areas, to be set up by the education ministry.

If the initiative is successful, and there is no reason to believe it will not be, this will serve to further reduce the number of students undertaking HE in the UK. Finally, the Browne Review may, as Sally Hunt, general secretary of the University and College Union argues, result in a drop in the number of overseas students, rather than in an influx. In particular, she warns that the reduced teaching budget at the heart of the coalition's plans 'will have a huge impact on the UK brand and the proud reputation we have on the global stage'. (Partridge, 2010).

If the UK is to continue to compete successfully for international students in a global market, and in turn reap the benefits of an international student cohort, it is important to have a good understanding of how satisfied international students are with all aspects of the university experience. This includes the quality of the teaching and learning with which they engage and the skills and knowledge they obtain as a result.

Key issues raised in the literature suggest that international students are often less engaged with the curriculum than their UK counterparts (Tompson & Tompson, 1996; Choi, 1997; Hellsten & Prescott, 2004; Krause et al 2005). While it is occasionally suggested that international students are passive learners and not intellectually or critically engaged in course material (Chalmers and Volet, 1997), other research suggests that this may be due to feelings of awkwardness (Krause et al, 2005), unrealistic expectations about the UK education system (Chalmers & Volet, 1997), language difficulties (Hellsten & Prescott, 2004) and the need to make massive social and cultural adjustments. In this context, Bamford (2008) points out that institutions have an academic and social responsibility to design learning environments which foster students' development in intercultural adaptability.

In summary, if we are to continually review and update our world position as a highly respected provider of education, UK HEIs must progress curriculum content and quality, constantly enhance the student experience, develop staff understanding and ensure all graduates are equipped with the requisite skills, knowledge, competence and confidence to enable them to make an impact in the world of work.

Research method

This chapter is based on the findings of research projects which sought to uncover the reality of perceptions and expectations from the perspective of the students and employers. There were four specific but interrelated research projects which focused on the four stages of the postgraduate educational life cycle:

❏ before study (part one)
❏ during study (part two)
❏ after study (part three)

❏ employment (part four)

Using semi-structured interviews and a phenomenographic approach to data analysis, the aim of part one was to elicit expectations of UK postgraduate education prior to student arrival. Interviews were undertaken in India with ten graduates who had applied to study in the UK. Part two involved ten international students maintaining an individual diary in which they recorded their lived experiences as they studied here in the UK. Part three focused on the reflected experiences of ten UK graduates in full time employment in India. Part four involved twenty semi-structured interviews with employers, primarily from Ghana and India. The focus was to determine the knowledge, skills, attributes and abilities sought from UK graduates by international employers.

Research findings

Part one Before study

Part one of the research reinforced anecdotal expectations. For example, the basis of the decision to study in the UK was heavily influenced by ranking tables:

> I am very brand conscious so I used the ranking tables to select the best place to do
> an MBA. The agent also helped make the decision.

However, understanding about what the different rankings actually meant was limited, as reference was frequently made to rankings that reflected undergraduate, rather than postgraduate, provision. In addition, few students were aware of the Research Assessment Exercise (RAE) or Research Excellence Framework (REF) as indicators of university excellence. Students were also influenced by the duration of the programme, preferring the one-year masters offered in the UK:

> My main reason for wanting to study law in the UK is that the course is much

Figure 3.1
The De Montfort stand generates interest at a graduate recruitment fair in India
(*Julia Pointon*)

shorter than in India – the undergraduate course is three years rather than five years, and the postgraduate part is one year rather than two, so I'm saving three years of my life when I can pursue many other things.

The majority of students accessed the services of agents to support their application and although many of the agents' counsellors are UK alumni, the opportunity to gain comprehensive information on possible differences in teaching and learning were restricted due to the time available. The consequence was that they were unaware of and relatively unprepared for the conventions of UK academic life and had given little thought to what life would be like. Some had an expectation that UK education would be far more practical in its orientation than they had experienced thus far:

> I think that the course in the UK is much more practical (for example, court room practice) whereas in India it is more theoretical and I would spend the first few years just writing in books.

Beyond very basic assumptions, detailed conceptions about the process of education remained vague and somewhat distant. The majority expected the experience to be the same as they had received to date. There was no consideration, for example, given to possible differences in academic writing conventions, teaching styles or assessment strategies. This is significant, because the dominant teaching style in India is didactic, with the lecturer arriving to teach the class and then leaving. Informal interaction with faculty is not the norm and consequently, when in the UK, students are sometimes reluctant to approach staff and seek advice or guidance.

> In India lecturers are recruited purely for their competence in the subject, whereas in the UK they are more friendly, less strict and more 'emancipated'.

> Lectures in India focus on one or two key texts which are followed chapter by chapter; handouts provide the student with the essential information they are required to learn, and examinations assess the extent to which they are able to 'give back' the learning.

> In India, you need to go by the book to pass exams, not your understanding.

Individual essay writing, reports, dissertations, group work or presentations are not the norm. Therefore, when students are asked to discuss issues, critically evaluate or analyse material they find it hard – as this, for many, is the first time they have been required to participate in such a learning process.

> In Madras we had about 150 students in a lecture, no handouts are given and we have one textbook for each subject. Students would quite often chat to each other throughout the lectures and then just study for the exams about one month before. It is routine practice to get notes from past students who have 'passed out' (for boys – not girls who go to all the lectures and write their own notes). There are some cases of 'chasing' which involves giving university people 2,000/3,000 Rupees to get a higher exam mark.

This fact alone underpins the central need to ensure students are provided with opportunities to learn how to learn, understand what we are doing in our approach to delivery and most crucially, why we are engaging with different approaches.

Agents played a vital role in supporting students in making their decision. The close links established between certain universities and agents was a strong influencing factor in their choice of institution. Ensuring that agents were fully briefed about the university programmes and teaching strategy emerged as an important feature in helping to ensure students were fully apprised of what to expect.

The number of direct applications is increasing, and some agents are concerned that their role will decline considerably over the forthcoming years. From an institutional perspective this emerging trend is noteworthy as it emphasises the need to provide additional information online. Finally, the research drew attention to the need for the host universities to ensure that appropriate pre-departure arrangements have been made and that immediate support on what to expect and how to manage their life as a student in the UK would be available.

The findings alert us to the need to:

❑ Undertake a comprehensive and strategic review of the nature and content of pre-departure information.

❑ Review working arrangements with agents, recognising their current role and the strategic implications associated with an anticipated decline in their centrality in the application process.

❑ To integrate marketing, applications and admissions processes to more accurately meet the needs of an independent IT-literate population whose primary information source is web-based.

❑ To enhance and develop the role of institutional alumni to ensure students have access to a 'voice' of experience.

Part two   During study

This stage of the research highlighted cultural and social pressures which affected the postgraduate students' ability and motivation to study:

> I felt frightened when I arrived in the UK for the first time. It is a strange country to me. So I did not know what to do in the first time although I had prepared everything......... I still felt nervous until the next day.

It became apparent that issues relating to loneliness, home life, underpinned by a lack of financial and home security, adversely affected their ability to progress and succeed in their chosen studies:

> The first week in Leicester, I didn't know many ways how to contact home; I just sent e-mail to my mum from the library computer network. There is no internet connection at my first month accommodation, Grange Court. There is only one public phone available at the ground floor for sharing with the other students of the whole building. So it seemed like I went away into the forest instead of studying abroad because it was difficult to contact back home during that time

> When I study in the UK there are some problems I have faced until now. The first

issue is discrimination, although UK is a democratic country there are some people still treat you in different attitude or let you suffer the danger situation, especially from teenagers. Some of my friends had been suffering the violence because of the different skin colour, so I must take note of security.

When I arrived in Leicester, my friend who studied here last year told me that some British people threw eggs to him when they drove pass by him. In my impression, British people are gentle and friendly to others. It is hard to believe that they could do that kind of things to others. But the few days before, when I stood behind the road to wait to the traffic light, someone driving pass by me and spit to me. It is disgusting. I cannot believe this would happen on me. I was very angry and disappointed.

As a consequence feelings of vulnerability and insecurity often prompted them to seek solace among their own compatriots:

In India we live with our parents until we are married but in the UK I will experience the freedom of living on my own. I would expect to be living in a hostel with Indian and British students but I would talk to the other Indians first.

The diaries reflected some of the struggles the students experienced in trying to adjust to new ways of learning:

UK teaching style is quite different from my country. In Thailand, we do not have many group discussions during the session because of the time consuming. In UK, when the tutor asked about the opinion I could not express it immediately because I had to translate the question and think about it; sometime I had the same idea as other students but my process was slower than them, so when they already answered I just kept quiet. Some tutors encouraged international students to participate in class by sharing about the same issue in their own country, this method made me felt more confident to express it.

Sadly, the diaries also included other entries which spoke of racism and bullying and underpinned the need for the host institutions to remain vigilant in identifying and dealing with such issues.

The findings alert us to the need to:

❑ Recognise that issues relating to home life, loneliness, financial insecurity, bullying and discrimination are real and adversely affect students' ability to progress and succeed in their chosen studies.

❑ Ensure that the host institutions remain vigilant in identifying and dealing with such issues, by reviewing and monitoring current arrangements, in particular for late enrollers.

❑ To undertake a rolling programme of awareness-raising of the issues among academic and non-academic staff.

Part three After study
This part brought to the fore very positive reflections of time spent in the UK.

Postgraduates identified a level of self-reliance, personal self-confidence and maturity they suggested they would not otherwise have realised. They reflected on their enhanced business skills, for example those of communication, team working, time management and report writing, and on the benefits derived from an international exposure to multiple cultures and lifestyles.

However, their reflections also included reference to the continuing Western focus of the curricula, and – despite the frequent use of module and programme labels which contained the words 'international', 'global' or 'multicultural' – the graduates considered the material they received to be UK or US-focused and did not regard it as representing an internationalised postgraduate curriculum:

> We come to the UK for international exposure not for the Western theory.

It also highlighted issues associated with reintegration into their home country. For many HEIs, the focus is on supporting students' entry to the UK, with little, if any regard for the problems they may face on returning to their homes:

> On returning to India it took me about six months to integrate and adapt back to my home culture. On reflection I really enjoyed the freedom of the student lifestyle in the UK and the whole experience has increased my confidence.

> My parents sent me to the UK to study because they hoped it would help my marriage prospects when I came back to India. But, I fear it has done the reverse. When I left I was a typical Indian girl, quiet, reserved and very respectful of my family. But now I see things differently. I am stronger, more sure of myself. I see there is a world out there with many interesting things and people. I want to be a part of that. I am not sure I can now marry an Indian man and be just his wife and a mother to his children.

The findings alert us to the need to:

❏ Audit current curriculum provision across all schools and faculties to ensure softer graduate attributes and skills are fully embedded.

❏ Hold as a strategic aspect of policy development in relation to Teaching Learning and Assessment that a non-Western curriculum is an expected element of taught provision.

❏ Develop learning and assessment activities that reflect both graduate skills and international dimensions of learning.

❏ Evolve specific postgraduate 'reintegration' support for students returning home through greater use of international alumni.

Part four Employment

This final stage involved twenty interviews with a range of companies in India and Ghana (see Plates 3 and 4). Representation was sought from the public and private sectors and included Public Service Commission, Black Star, Barclays, ABP Consultants, Standard Chartered and Tigo Communications. All recruited graduates from the UK. There was a remarkable level of agreement among the employers in

Figure 3.2
Mature students at a
recruitment event in
Cambodia
(*Julia Pointon*)

terms of the impact they sought from postgraduates.

For graduates to have impact they needed to have a high level of competence and capability in personal professionalism as well as in emotional and social intelligence. Employers looked for evidence that the students had engaged in activities beyond the taught curriculum and that such programmes were to be encouraged and certificated. They sought graduates who could be critical in their appraisal of work situations, and could show that they had developed the capacity to engage with lifelong learning, along with the ability to generate and transfer knowledge. They were concerned with demonstration of the ability to operate as a member of a team, and contribute according to experience.

Equally employers valued highly the skills developed through masters level research and report writing. The advice was to ensure all students had exposure to financial, strategic and risk management, as this level of understanding and capability is crucial in countries where political and social turbulence provide a unique context for business operations. Employers were firmly of the view that a UK graduate has the necessary impact to be successful when they return home and that they do bring different understandings, insights and observations which leverage and build organisational capacity. They noted, however, that the UK curriculum continues to be Western in its orientation.

Generally, employers commented that wider use of examples from other countries to better reflect the wider international business agenda would be helpful to home and international students alike. All companies contacted indicated a strong willingness to partner UK educational institutions to collaborate in developing appropriate case studies or problem based scenarios designed to enrich and extend the focus of the curriculum.

The findings alert us to the need to:

❏ Develop additional programmes and activities to support personal growth and learning. Volunteering or service-learning models provide a suitable framework. Accreditation and formal recognition for skills development in valued in both Ghana and India.

❏ Seek to extend international collaboration and partnerships with employers who are representative of students' country of origin. Writing joint case studies, using real life examples, provides the students with an understanding of business in other cultures and offers a balance in curriculum focus.

❏ Note the fact that employers did not seek specific vocational expertise, rather the demonstration of the ability to operate as a member of a team and contribute according to experience.

Conclusions

Coming to a new and foreign country is often an exciting event which is rich with potential. However, the experience can be coloured by uncertainty and disorientation when a student is faced with a new culture and new social as well as academic expectations. Shifting from familiar to unfamiliar learning environments, the students profiled in this research have undergone a series of educational, social and personal transitions. Indeed, their transition continues beyond their return to the home country.

This work was inspired by conversations with international students and their lecturers who identified a 'poor fit' between the expectations held by international students before starting studies in the UK and their actual experiences while studying. The research determined that in many instances students did not have any clear understanding of UK academic conventions or how these might affect their experiences of studying in the UK. The main lesson learned is that institutions should ensure the provision of full information for prospective applicants and that they should use existing country networks to ensure the effective 'translation' of this information.

The research next considered what students encountered in their lives in the UK. It determined the extent to which personal issues, such as the difficulty of assimilating in a new country with a different cultural context, influenced the students' experience. Language, climate and social conventions posed a series of challenges which often adversely affected their ability to study. The key learning point is that all institutions need to ensure that the social and personal support systems they offer are sufficient to support a wide range of non-academic needs.

Experiences of students returning to their home country and gaining full time employment highlighted the most valued aspects of what they had acquired – soft skills rather than simply pure academic knowledge. The graduates spoke of the extent to which their ability to make an impact was underpinned by their development of effective communication skills, their personal growth and enhanced independence, and the improvement in their professional attitude and competence.

The final part of the research focused on the needs of employers and draws attention to their search to recruit graduates who could make a difference to their business operations by adding internal value. They seek graduates who can demonstrate academic awareness combined with a high level of personal and professional confidence and maturity. The graduates with most impact are those who possessed clear business acumen, are able to think laterally, challenge the status quo and demonstrate cultural sensitivity. The research has served to focus the activities of HEIs to ensure a more holistic approach to initial recruitment of students from overseas, the provision of effective pastoral and personal support facilities, the recognition of the importance of providing opportunities to develop 'soft' life skills, and the need to support graduates' reintegration and new employment in their home countries.

References

Bamford, J. (2008) Improving International Students' experience of studying in the UK: A case study of international student experience. London Metropolitan Business School. http://www.economic-snetwork.ac.uk/showcase/bamford_international.htm

Chalmers, D., & Volet, S. (1997) Common misconceptions about students from South-East Asia studying in Australia. *Higher Education Research and Development* 16 (1) 87–98

Choi, M. (1997) Korean students in Australian universities: Intercultural issues. *Higher Education Research and Development* 16 (3) 263–82

Hellsten, M., & Prescott, A. (2004) Learning at university: The international student experience. *International Education Journal* 5 (3) 344–51

Krause, K.L., Hartley, R., James, R. & McInnis, C. (2005) The first year experience in Australian universities: Findings from a decade of national studies. Retrieved 16 October 2006 from http://www.cshe.unimelb.edu.au/downloads/FYEReport05KLK.pdf

Partridge, M. (2010) Mixed Reception. *Times Higher Education* December

Tompson, H. B., & Tompson, G. H. (1996) Confronting diversity issues in the classroom with strategies to improve satisfaction and retention of international students. Journal of Education for Business Sep/Oct 72 (53) 57

Universities UK (UUK) (2009) Higher Education in Facts and Figures, Summer 2009. Accessed 28 March 2011 from http://www.universitiesuk.ac.uk/Publications/Documents/Facts09.pdf

University World News (28 February 2011) p1

JULIA POINTON works in human resource management and organisational studies where she combines academic management with a strong interest in the practice of learning and teaching in higher education. She is involved in curriculum and programme development, teaching, research and in working with an extensive range of external international partners and stakeholders. She is principal lecturer and programme director in the Business School at DeMontfort University, where her work provides a national focus for institutional teaching and learning excellence for international students. With financial support from the Higher Education Academy BMAF subject centre, Julia has led the establishment of their internationalisation special interest group.

4

The world of work concept (WoW®) and student curriculum experience

Sarah Nixon and Terry Dray
Liverpool John Moores University

Developing graduates who are self-reflective, able to sell themselves and highly employable is the challenge for higher education. This chapter explores a solution which is both a university strategy and a programme-level operational process and which has changed the way the staff work and the students are supported.

Context and rationale

Liverpool John Moores University (LJMU) has a lengthy track record of vocational excellence, with significant existing links and contacts with employers and organisations in the regional, national and international arena. The World of Work (WoW®) programme was established in 2007 as a strategic response to the challenges from growth in the higher education (HE) sector which included: increasing competition in the region from other HE institutions (HEI); the increasing competitiveness of the graduate job recruitment market; and consistent employer feedback that students have a poor understanding of the job market.

> Employers generally see a graduate's achievements related to the subject discipline as necessary but not sufficient for them to be recruited. In some employment contexts the actual subject discipline may be relatively unimportant. Achievements outside the boundaries of the discipline (such as the possession of so-called 'soft skills') are generally considered to be important in the recruitment of graduates (Yorke 2006).

Most HEIs in the UK would claim to develop skills relevant to future employment and often have developed additional, small-scale, or 'bolt-on' activities to boost the employability prospects of their graduates. LJMU has taken a different, more radical approach which can be summarised as 'connecting both students and staff more closely to the World of Work' (LJMU, 2007). The unique element of this strategy is the role of employers, who are working in partnership with the university in defining and verifying employment-related skills. Alongside this the students are working towards a separate accreditation where they start to define their own development, skills, knowledge and experience.

The programme focused on here is a traditional, semi-vocational, three-year undergraduate degree in Sport Development with an intake of 80 students per year. What happens to the students on graduation has gained importance at a programme level over the last few years. It was no longer good enough just to focus on their degree programme – a longer-term focus was needed. Although the staff knew the skills, knowledge and ability that students had in their repertoire, on the whole the students themselves were not able to express them, and had difficulty selling themselves to possible employers. The WoW® programme has been an excellent way of focusing the curriculum and the students on the needs of graduates once they enter the job market. The university agenda has had an impact on the programme in a number of ways:

❏ increased involvement with external employers
❏ developed links to outside organisations for work related learning
❏ students focusing on their understanding of themselves and the workplace they
   want to work in, through personal development planning (PDP).

One of the students who went through the WoW® process and who presently is training to be a teacher comments that:

> As soon as I learned about WoW and its benefits I knew it was worth pursuing. The graduate job market is extremely competitive at the moment and any opportunity, no matter how small, to 'get ahead' should be seized. But that wouldn't be doing the WoW certificate justice – it's a big opportunity to have that something extra to take to employers. It has left me feeling confident about my ability, focused in my aspirations and prepared to achieve what I want in life.

Description

The strategic aim of WoW® is to deliver for our students a high-quality academic programme connected to the world of work and business and to develop graduates who will not require long 'learning curves' when they start employment (Mason, Williams and Cranmer 2006). LJMU has faced this challenge by addressing graduate and transferable skills, and now provides a programme that ensures graduates will closely match what employers are looking for.

Recognising the need for transferable skills and competences is about establishing a sense of 'employability' in graduates. By working in consultation with employers, students and staff at LJMU we have provided a credible and robust programme of employability. Turning an intangible concept into something concrete has been the focus of over five years of research and consultation on employability and has led to successful delivery of the World of Work employability programme and certificate. The programme has helped to create graduates who can enter the workplace and make a direct impact: they know about themselves, they understand organisations and they can make things happen.

What does this mean in practice? All degree programmes in LJMU now have to have an element of **work-related learning**; students therefore have a chance to engage with the external world and impact on it. One of the objectives of WoW® is to bring students and staff closer to the world of work. There are many different approaches that can be taken and consequently through WoW® a range of opportunities are on offer for students to engage with external agencies, speakers and events. Through the university brokerage service vast numbers of opportunities are available to students who wish to go out and get experience working in organisations of their choice, and programmes are also supported in finding placements for their students. A student comments:

> I was unsure about what to expect out of the placement but that has gone so well that it's made me want to get as much as possible out of university, not just from my course, but to make sure that I'm prepared for the workplace after university and to build up my portfolio.

The WoW® in Conversation Programme brings in key speakers from the world of work to share experiences of the modern workplace and the challenges of developing organisations and leadership. Speakers have included Philip Green, CEO United Utilities; Gill Palmer, vice-president Oracle Corporation; Denise Barret-Baxendale, CEO The Everton Foundation and Julie Ridley, a Marks & Spencer store manager. A work-related-learning fair is now offered annually for students to engage with not-for-profit organisations to develop collaborations for dissertations and research projects. One employer noted that:

> the quality of preparation has increased this year in the students applying for gap-year placements and this seems to be down to the WoW® process.

Another element of the overall WoW® agenda relates to the individual students ability to recognise their uniqueness and to reflect on this for an external audience. One of the difficulties as students turn into graduates is their explicit knowledge of what they have done and what they can do; this helps them to articulate their skills and abilities and sell themselves to employers. This process has three parts which have been matched against the needs of employers and how job applications can be constructed. The students have to submit personal accounts in relation to their:

❏ self-awareness
❏ organisational awareness
❏ making things happen.

On completion of these three stages the student is invited for an interview with an external interviewer in which they get a chance to get feedback on how they have done. One of the past students, who is now in a graduate job, was not successful in this interview on the first attempt and commented that

> The interview for WoW® was really important. I went in not sure what I was doing and messed it up. The feedback I got was excellent and I know now what I need to do when I go for my first proper job, how to dress, how to behave and what to say.

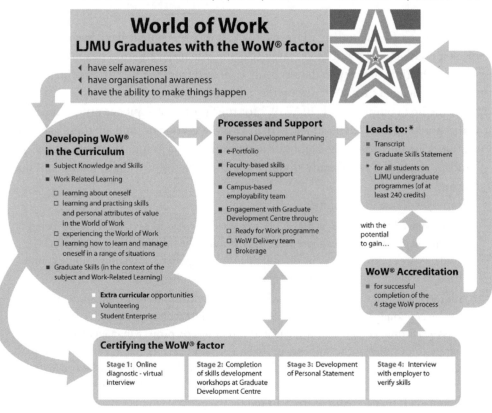

Figure 4.1 The WoW® Process at Liverpool John Moores University

The WoW® approach we describe here encompasses the whole university experience and students' personal development while studying and beyond (see Figure 1). Through their involvement with the process, students should be able to enter the workplace with the skills needed to both do the current job and also progress in their career. An understanding of self and an awareness of the environment should help the graduates ensure a best fit for them as individuals with their career choices. Throughout the process, the aim is to ensure graduates can enter the workplace, make a direct impact and be able to reflect and build on this. It is too early to say how much long-term impact WoW® will have, but both staff and employers are reporting that they can see a difference.

> The WoW programme was something I only became familiar with in my final year of study. I felt that it looked to be an ideal opportunity for me to develop skills that would be required within the working world. I am thrilled that I have had this opportunity to complete all stages of the WoW programme as it has allowed me to prepare and focus on different elements that are required when applying for jobs. (Sports development student)

Evaluation

WoW® is open to all students. However, levels of engagement have been varied. As this is a relatively new initiative, large-scale university evaluation has not yet taken place. At the time of writing, data is being collected from the more than 800 students who have engaged in WoW® during the year 2009–10.

For the first complete cycle of WoW® for the Sport Development programme 15% of the graduates in 2010 achieved their WoW® certificate and of these 80% are now working in graduate level jobs or undertaking post-graduate qualifications. The numbers engaged have already doubled for the next cohort and interest continues to grow.

Employers have commented:

> I interviewed three students all of whom passed with good reviews with one being exceptional. I didn't know there were opportunities like this for students and LJMU students are so fortunate to be offered this WoW experience, would willingly come back to conduct further interviews. (Senior manager, Royal Mail)

> I interviewed four students all of whom passed with one highly exceptional and two exceptional interviewees. There was a star interviewee who delivered a first-class performance and had a great understanding of project management. I was happy to put one of the students in touch with an HMP Forensic Psychologist as she wants to develop a career in this area. One of the students wanted to work in mental health. I was taken aback by her sincerity and wish to help the less fortunate. It was a breath of fresh air to talk to such a young person who wants to help make a big difference to others. (Prison Officer, HM Prison Service)

Discussion

Establishing a strategic employability approach is a complex task and the following are some examples of the activities.

❏ Reviewing relevant literature and canvassing opinion from relevant stakeholders, including academics and employers.

❏ Establishing a national Employer Advisory Group with major national and international employers to influence the skills agenda.

❏ Developing criteria that provide the basis for the three strands of WoW® (see Figure 1).

❏ Enlisting the support of local employers as verifiers of the WoW® certificate.

❏ Establishing key performance indicators across the university.

❏ Redefining careers-related provision already in place in the University.

❏ Acquiring resources, ranging from the physical 'building' – the Graduate Development Centre (GDC) – to the staff that support the WoW® programme, namely a delivery team, a brokerage team and an administration team.

❏ Vigorously marketing WoW® to students and academics.

❏ Delivery of the WoW® programme in each faculty through careers professionals.

❑ Developing processes for the collection and assessment of personal statements against the WoW® criteria.

Additionally, LJMU:

❑ Earmarked significant institutional funding over a five-year period.

❑ Recognised the importance of basic, practical skills related to the workplace and creating various opportunities for students to develop their capability in these areas.

❑ Developed a new HE support role – the Skills Support Officer – working with staff across the university in supporting students in their reflection and evidencing of employability potential and personal development planning

The strategic initiative has been translated at programme level in a number of ways:

Curriculum development

To integrate the processes into all three levels of study has involved the programme team looking at the modules where employability fits strongly: work-related learning modules, live projects, problem-based learning approaches. Across modules conversations happen in all sessions to integrate the learning and get the students to link and analyse both content and their own growth and development.

Personal development planning

In this structured process, students look at their own development, set goals, reflect, coach and mentor each other. The WoW® processes are built into this and are supported by a strong and well-established personal tutor system where feedback is used as a developmental tool.

Employability focus

Individuals from the relevant industries are brought in to talk to the students from Week One of their course, developing an understanding of what will be needed to ensure that they will be able to enter that industry in the future. The careers service is then used to support the students in developing their profile.

Summer 2010 saw the end of the first full year of offering the WoW® certificate. At this time 3,500 (15%) students were voluntarily registered on the WoW® certificate module and 833 (4%) WoW® certificate statements had been submitted. Over 11,000 (48%) students had participated in WoW®-related group work facilitated by graduate development staff and academics and a new university-wide vacancy system had received over 900 vacancies from 600 employers. Also, many examples of the WoW® certificate being integrated into academic programmes were established.

To celebrate the achievements of the WoW® students, a graduation ceremony was held for both the graduates and current students who had been successful in achieving their WoW® certification (see Plate 5).

One graduate of the Sport Development programme returned to talk to all current students as well as delivering at a university event on WoW®. She said that:

The job market is very challenging. I have just got my first job and was chosen out of 85 people that applied. Without having gone through the WoW® process I don't believe I would have got this job. I was very sceptical about spending time thinking about myself and what I can do but it was probably one of the most important things I did.

Barriers, challenges and lessons learned

Effective management, process development, and most importantly stakeholder engagement are essential to successfully implement strategic change like this. Effectively communicating the 'offer', including the aims, methods of engagement and outputs/benefits is essential. Employer partners were relatively easy to secure as WoW® is a unique labour market matching model which has been designed, developed and delivered with employers and resonates with those seeking to recruit talented graduates. Recruiting academic colleagues to champion the cause and act as influential advocates and drivers of the processes with their students has been essential; however, this has not always been easy. Academics need to see the value to these approaches and this has taken time. Early adopters and champions have been used to sell the message with some success. One colleague notes:

> Too many people think that our main priority is to fill the students' heads with information, not so me; I believe that we have a responsibility to prepare them for the job market in equal measures.

Engaging time-poor students in voluntary processes that many would prefer to put off and 'do tomorrow' is a continual challenge. At programme level the WoW® agenda has been difficult to establish as a useful exercise for students who do not yet know what the job market is like and what is needed to secure employment. As the numbers engaging continue to grow, and as the students start to talk to each other, this becomes a little easier. Academic staff are crucial in spreading the word and supporting the processes. Personal tutors and targeted modules have been used to engage the student body.

However, the students who have followed the process have found it useful and, in some situations, extremely valuable to them in securing a first position, as evidenced by the feedback quoted here. One graduate said that completing the WoW® certificate was 'life-changing'. These real life stories are now being used to help other students to gain an understanding of the importance of focusing on employability and developing themselves throughout their degree. For example, a graduate comments:

> Alongside the degree I did the WoW certificate and it's been brilliant. It's not over-exaggerating to say it got me my job. I am now a lecturer, but I could not have done it without WoW. LJMU and the WoW programme have literally changed my life and I'm really grateful for the support I've received.

If we were introducing this strategic programme again, greater emphasis would be placed on communicating earlier and more clearly how each of the elements – work related learning, graduate skills and WoW® certificate skills – are both complementary and differentiated. No assumptions would be made that people (academics and students) will 'just get it'.

Encouraging engagement with the WoW® skills certificate through integrating the process into academic programmes would also be prioritised earlier. As a means of encouraging academics and other faculty staff to see the relevance of the programme, earlier use would be made of factual data. For example, graduate destination statistics by academic programme could be shared with staff so they could see how many of their students are in graduate jobs. The more information that is shared the more connected academic programmes can be to the world of work, and the more understanding there will be of the necessity for graduates to go into work and make a difference.

Conclusion

The LJMU approach to creating graduates who can have impact has been developed through discussions and engagement with employers who bring their expertise into the university. Although it is early days to report overall impact, anecdotal evidence suggests that there is a growing engagement in the WoW® and employers are seeing a difference in the graduates they meet. The processes and programmes that are now delivered are focused on what employers want to see in graduates which creates, in turn, a strong link between how the student develops and what they will need to do on graduation.

References

Mason, G., Williams, G. and Cranmer, S. (2006) Employability Skills Initiatives in Higher Education: What Effects Do They Have On Graduate Labour Market Outcomes? *Education Economics* March 2009, **17** (1) 1-30

Yorke, M. (2006) *Employability in higher education: what it is – what it is not.* Learning and Employability Series 1. York: HEA

Liverpool John Moores University (LJMU 2007) Connecting both students and staff more closely to the World of Work (WoW). At www.ljmu.ac.uk/wow

SARAH NIXON is a principal lecturer in sport development within the Centre for Sport, Dance and Outdoor Education and the faculty learning development manager. Her main areas of research are personal development planning and the student experience.

TERRY DRAY is director of the Graduate Development Centre at Liverpool John Moores University, UK. His professional interests focus on student and graduate employability and career development. He is currently managing a WoW® certificate pilot project, funded by the Malaysian Government, at Universiti Teknolgi Mara (UiTM) – Malaysia's largest university.

5

Developing ethical thinking with undergraduates in sport and exercise science

Grace Robinson and Karen Llewellyn
University of Leeds

This chapter describes the development of ethical thinking in sport and exercise at the University of Leeds. We consider some of the ways in which this has been enhanced by the innovative work of Inter-Disciplinary Ethics Applied, the IDEA Centre for Excellence in Teaching and learning (CETL). Discussions with staff and students inform our reflection on the teaching and learning experience as well as the recommendations we make to anyone interested in developing the ethical thinking of their students and helping them to become graduates with impact in the world.

Our graduates will enter a world of ambiguity, uncertainty and change which Barnett describes as a world of 'super-complexity' (2000): in the context of undergraduate education we prepare students for futures not yet known. In this challenging context graduates have to be able to contribute to, rather than simply consume, knowledge, so students need to develop the appropriate cognitive skills for making sound ethical judgements, enabling them to be competent, responsible yet creative agents of change.

For example, graduates in the world of sport, as coaches, teachers, health professionals, managers, administrators or more obviously as performers, will be faced with ever-changing contexts where the previously accepted and known frameworks in which they operate are contested. This will require an increased individual response to particular actions, according to Barnett (2000). Further endorsement lies in the hospitality, leisure, sport and tourism subject area's (HLST) benchmark statements (QAA, 2008) which contain the aspiration that undergraduate students should be able recognise and respond to moral, ethical and safety issues which directly relate to the subject domain, including relevant legislation and professional codes of conduct.

Developing ethical thinking in undergraduates
The overarching aim of the IDEA CETL is to help students (and also professionals

40

and employees) to identify, analyse and respond to the ethical issues they encounter in their subject disciplines and their working lives. Their activities seek to raise the profile of ethics, not just at the University of Leeds but also throughout higher education and professional life.

The centre works with disciplines from across the university including biological sciences, business, computing, dentistry, engineering, environment, geography and transport, medicine, media and communications, nanotechnology. In sport and exercise sciences, as elsewhere, the centre has worked in partnership with academics and other experts to develop content and methodologies to embed sports ethics in the undergraduate sport and exercise programme. In sport and exercise science, this work began in September 2006.

The distinctive and effective features of this method are genuine 'inter-disciplinarity' and thorough integration. The centre works in partnership with colleagues from the host discipline to ensure that teaching is both properly grounded in subject practice and properly informed by the dialectical and conceptual skills required for engagement in ethics. It is neither philosophers preaching theory to professionals, nor professionals merely focusing on code compliance.

The content produced consists of relevant, subject-specific teaching resources built around case studies, vignettes and contemporary readings (See IDEA, 2008–present) Concurrently, generic resources were also developed to support those teaching ethics for the first time (see Athanassoulis, 2006).

Enabling aspects of the learning and teaching experience

Team-teaching and co-delivery

A key enabling feature of the learning and teaching experience at Leeds is the use of team teaching, where a lecturer/tutor from the host discipline works with an ethicist from the CETL to deliver a session. There are three main reasons for this.

❏ *Credibility*

If tutors from the host discipline participate in the 'ethics components' of the module the students can see that ethics is important to the discipline/profession as well as to ethicists.

❏ *Connectedness and proper integration*

The tutor from the host discipline will be able to connect the ethics components to other parts of the module/curriculum and thus ensure the ethical issues are appropriately integrated into their module and/or programme.

❏ *Relevant skills*

An ethics tutor teaching alone may be unable to answer discipline-specific questions raised; conversely, a tutor from the host discipline with little or no experience of ethics may be unable to probe ethical issues or respond more deeply.

The involvement of an ethicist

In general, ethical thinking is done much more clearly and carefully when a philosopher/ethicist is involved. This is precisely because of their awareness of what has been covered in the philosophical tradition of ethics. Sometimes this is a matter of greater caution in endorsing over-ambitious ethical conclusions. Sometimes it is a matter of seeing how progress can be made on an issue that seems intractable to non-philosophers.

Philosophers address these ethical issues from a different perspective. Students are likely to benefit more broadly from learning to think in different ways.

The use of case studies and vignettes

Despite the theoretical grounding of their tutors, IDEA's approach to ethics does not typically involve teaching students ethical theories. Instead they approach ethical issues through case studies and vignettes, which ground issues in the study and practice of the host discipline.

The use of case studies encourages students to consider ethical issues as part of a holistic assessment of a particular situation. For example, in their first year students at Leeds are asked: Should we hothouse children from an early age to improve our chances of international sporting success?

To address this issue they are asked to consider the case of Dominique Moceanu, a child gymnast who sued for legal emancipation from her parents in 1998. The students addressing this case are required to consider a range of empirical questions such as: How does intense training affect a child's body? Are children more prone to injury than adults? How do children cope with the psychological stress of intense training?

But alongside these questions the students are encouraged to draw out relevant philosophical questions, for example: Why is winning valuable? Who should make decisions for children? Are children competent to consent to participate in these programmes? Is hot-housing abusive? Students who explore ethical issues in this way are better equipped to identify, analyse and respond to ethical issues where they arise in the real world.

Independent learning

One of the central skills of philosophical ethics is thinking through an issue for one's self, not having the answer given by a tutor or book. In sport and exercise science, students explore ethical issues using small group discussions supported by focused study questions. The tutor's role is to facilitate independent thought by:

❏ Asking and inviting *further questions*
❏ Identifying, forming and inviting students to form *hypotheses*
❏ Asking for *reasons*

- ❏ Asking for (and providing) *examples and counter examples*
- ❏ Identifying (and sometimes making) *distinctions*
- ❏ Identifying (and sometimes making) *connections*
- ❏ Exploring implications; asking for (and sometimes providing) *criteria*
- ❏ Asking for *consistency* and exposing *inconsistency*
- ❏ Introducing *additional considerations*.

Tutors make it clear to students that they expect them to arrive at justified, defensible conclusions. All students can benefit from learning to think for themselves.

The context of the learning and teaching experience

Context of sport ethics at Leeds

Sport and Exercise Science (SES) students at Leeds cover four curriculum areas during their programme of study; biomechanics, physiology, psychology, and motor control. Graduates from the programme pursue a range of careers; some directly related to sport and exercise science (such as physiotherapy, sports psychology and PE teaching) and others not, such as the police, fire services and the armed forces. The materials taught at first year undergraduate level (Level 4) are designed to complement the curriculum content and remain broadly relevant to a range of future sport-related careers.

Design of the integrated applied-ethics components of this course began in 2005 with the formation of an SES Ethics Theme Team. The SES Ethics Theme Team is one of a network of steering groups including academic staff from the host discipline (including enthusiasts and decision-makers), student representatives, ethicists from the IDEA CETL, a representative of another ethics-theme team and an administrator from the CETL. This team met in various forms up to six times a year and informed all aspects of curriculum development, delivery and evaluation.

The teaching of sport ethics

Teaching of sport ethics at Leeds began in September 2006 with four pilot seminars in a *Study Skills* module, covering an introduction to ethics. The module explored the ethics of hazing (initiation ceremonies) to coincide with the student's first weeks at university, the ethics of plagiarism, the ethics of teamwork and the ethics of coaching children. These seminars were complemented by an *Introduction to Ethics* lecture and a summary lecture. The sessions were team-taught by the module leader, a SES lecturer and an ethicist; 150 first-year undergraduate (Level 4) students were taught in groups of thirty on a carousel model.

In 2007 we began teaching for second-year undergraduates (Level 5). Students undertook seminars in research ethics in anticipation of their final year dissertation as part of the module on *Research Design, Implementation and Analysis*. The research ethics covered were in the areas of confidentiality and informed consent.

Curriculum content

Ethics of initiations

The students' first experience of ethics concerned issues surrounding sport-related initiations and pranks. This session was timed to coincide with fresher's week – a time when some students may encounter these issues as part of their memberships of teams and sports clubs.

The session introduced some of the arguments used to defend these practices and some of the arguments used to condemn them, prompting discussion of risk, harm, consent and responsibility. Students explored these issues through small group discussion around a series of case studies; while also drawing on their own experiences or those of their peers using video examples from YouTube as a stimulus for discussion.

Ethics of plagiarism

The next in the seminar series considered issues around academic integrity delivered in conjunction with practical guidance about presentation and referencing of academic work. This seminar involved a conceptual analysis of plagiarism which highlighted distinctive features and explained why it might be considered unethical, namely its unfairness, the dishonesty involved and its contrariness to the purpose of academic study. Risk to institutional integrity, if this is not taken seriously by a university, was a further emerging issue for discussion.

Parallels were made during this session to cheating in sport, drawing on the similarities with academic cheating and plagiarism, in terms of possible threats to the 'spirit of sport'. A consequence of this interrogation was to contest particular assessment strategies which lent themselves more readily to acts of plagiarism and a discussion of alternative but equally rigorous modes of assessment less likely to encourage such acts.

Ethics of teamwork

Using a collection of hypothetical vignettes and discussion questions, the third session in the series considered individual and collective responsibility, shared aims, team discipline and the problem of free riders; loyalty and faithfulness and collective praise and blame.

Sporting examples were used to demonstrate key themes, for example, hypothetical scenarios, students' own experiences of individual and team activities as well as high-profile cases in sport, for example, Roy Keane (football) in relation to team discipline and Kevin Pietersen (cricket) in relation to team loyalty.

Ethics of coaching children

The final seminar for first-year undergraduates (Level 4) considered intense training and elitism in sport. The seminar was based around case studies from contemporary news reports; the first of which concerned the young gymnast mentioned above, Dominique Moceanu, who sued for legal emancipation from her parents in 1998. A problem-based learning model was adopted in this seminar, with students encouraged to generate empirical and philosophical questions about the case. Their questions formed the basis of their subsequent discussions, supported by study questions.

Assessment

Initially the ethical components at Leeds were not assessed; the course requirements of students were simply attendance, and reasonable levels of participation during discussions. In 2008 we trialled assessments designed to mimic the format of existing first-year (Level 4) study-skills assessments; multiple-choice questions and short written responses and extended essay questions. While much of the philosophical curriculum content did not lend itself to a multiple-choice format, aspects of the course, such as best practice when obtaining informed consent, did.

In 2008, students were assessed in this way on a number of factors, including appropriate disclosure of information, appropriate means of communication and indicators of competence

In the following example, bold indicates the correct answer:

Q1. Which of the following factors could justify your judgement that an individual is **not competent** to give informed consent? (tick all that apply)
- **The individual is five years old**
- The individual is over 60
- **The individual seems agitated or upset**
- The individual is devoutly religious
- The individual seems arrogant
- **The individual has dementia**
- **The individual has been drinking**
- The individual has a history of mild depression
- **You suspect the individual has not understood the information given**
- The individual is under 18.

Extended essay questions focused on case studies; students were asked to assume the perspective of a range of individuals in positions of responsibility in a sport-related context. For example, the director of an exercise physiology laboratory that provides exercise-testing of people following a heart attack, or the senior coach for the Leeds Junior Swimming Club. Students were assessed on their ability to identify relevant ethical issues that might face such a person, explain the significance of such issues and comment on their relation to other ethical considerations. Finally they were invited to suggest 'best practice'.

From 2009, these case studies became the main focus for student assessment. Essays were replaced by group research projects and in-class presentations. This allowed students to further develop a range of study skills while exploring an issue in an open-ended, dialectic manner better suited to the complexity of the issues.

The barriers and challenges to effective learning

Introducing ethics

Often students are unfamiliar with the term 'ethics' or with ethical issues from their discipline or the wider world. Asking a class what they understand by 'ethics' and 'morality' was often a good place to start.

Motivating students' learning in ethics

Sometimes tutors of ethics have encountered resistance among students (and occasionally staff) to the inclusion of ethics in their programme of study. Individuals in the host discipline may have mixed feelings about our involvement as 'outsiders'. Some students may consider ethical decision-making to be a personal matter or simply a matter of common sense. Some students may suspect that ethics tutors are there to admonish them or tell them how to behave. Some students will be sceptical about the relevance of ethics to their discipline.

In anticipation of these issues, the IDEA tutors found it helpful to begin sessions with some introductory remarks on the role of an ethics tutor and the nature of applied ethics in their discipline. Sometimes students were encouraged to suggest areas of ethical enquiry in their discipline.

Encouraging debate

In some classes, students made up their minds very quickly and having done so felt as though they had dealt with an issue and were ready to move on. In other classes students came quickly to a consensus on an issue and as a result, seemed reluctant to consider opposing views. In situations like these, discussion can dry up.

One approach to such situations is to assume the 'devil's advocate' position yourself, bringing in further considerations and asking students to defend their views in light of what you have said.

While this can be very effective, tutors at the CETL have emphasised the importance of uncovering genuine disagreement *in the group* and placing the onus on the students to critically engage with one another's views. During the ethics teaching at Leeds this has been achieved by identifying points of difference, or inconsistencies between students' contributions. For example, some students may agree on a point, but for different reasons, or they may agree broadly but differ on the detail.

Where there appears to be little genuine disagreement between members of the group we often simply asked: what would someone who disagreed with you say?

Ethics and law

A key objective for our tutors was to support students in recognising the difference between ethics and the law. In initial sessions we typically found that some students would seek clarification of the legal basis for certain actions before condemning the illegal and condoning the legal.

Case studies were particularly useful in such instances; particularly the case of Muhammad Ali's 1967 appeal for conscientious-objector status – an appeal turned down by the Justice Department for failing to meet legal requirements (a case of ethical law breaking?) and the 1996 case in which an Indian associate of the British American Tobacco group sponsored the Indian World Cup Cricket (a case of legal, yet unethical, behaviour?)

Ethicists were careful to point out to students that they were not experts on the legal aspects of cases; nonetheless, students did sometime seek guidance on the law. Where we felt it was relevant, our teaching was enhanced by supplementary information for students on the legal aspects and implications of cases.

The student experience
The effectiveness and appropriateness of the learning experience

Before the introduction of the ethics component for first-year (Level 4) undergraduates study-skills students had reported some misgivings about the relevance of material included in this module. Consequently the module leader was keen to demonstrate that ethical reasoning and critical thinking were vital skills for their discipline studies and future careers.

Feedback from course evaluation questionnaires in 2009 suggested that in most cases these skills were highly valued by students. Many students felt the ethics components enabled them to 'consider more aspects of an issue before jumping to your initial view' acknowledging that they often took 'a more open view on issues' as a result.

The positive aspects of their experience were derived from learning 'differently' from other parts of their degree programme.

On the whole students favoured the more enquiry-led, discursive approaches which focused on ethical questions. Particular advantages observed by students were the opportunities to listen to the ethical positions of others in small group discussions, the chance to articulate a well-structured argument and increased confidence in expressing a viewpoint.

The interactive nature of the seminars was well-received by most students, with some acknowledging that by learning in such a way 'you think about things that you might not have thought about if you were learning alone.'

Students were more motivated to engage in discussion when ethical issues directly related to the sports context. Some students felt that issues concerning academic integrity, while relevant to their personal lives, were not sufficiently relevant to the study of sport and their future careers.

Feedback in the early stages of this pilot also suggested that while they enjoyed the discussions, a significant number of students felt they lasted too long. This was a concern the course designers had to balance against the importance of giving students space to explore the issues in sufficient depth. In some cases students of all disciplines may be inclined to take a fairly superficial view of ethical issues and where this is the case, time is needed to illuminate the complexity. This was possible for some students: 'I learnt to think in more depth about questions I thought were simple.' '[I learnt] that what I think and believe should be challenged; there are often two sides to an argument.'

Lessons learned

Staff perspective

❏ Staff perceived significant benefits in contextualising ethical content in hypothetical, real-life and personal sport-related scenarios. Where this took place students found the learning more meaningful.

❏ Small group discussions facilitated greater inclusion and involvement in the predominantly enquiry-led, discursive mode of learning

❏ Staff felt the use of case studies was a highly effective means by which to promote dialogue and enquiry around key ethical issues.

Student perspective

Students developed an awareness of how and where ethical issues might fit into their subject with many suggesting further areas of enquiry in their feedback.

Students widely reported the benefits of exploring an issue through constructive group discussion; recognising, in particular, the value of other people's views. Students found sport-related, 'real life' case studies. Those presented in printed and digital media were particularly engaging.

In conclusion

The teaching of ethics in the context of sport and exercise at undergraduate level clearly is not without its challenges. However, student evaluations reveal that the more the ethical content relates to undergraduate experiences, the greater the engagement; adopting a case study approach only serves to enhance this engagement. It is unsurprising that we should advocate the inclusion of teaching ethics in the undergraduate sport and exercise curriculum, for the reasons previously mentioned.

It is apparent from the embedding of ethics teaching that students move beyond relativist positions ('well, it's just a matter of opinion') or an over-reliance on legal positions ('it's against the law so it must be wrong') to more sophisticated, independent positions. As a consequence this significantly enhances graduates' capacities to make sound, ethical judgements in both their personal and professional lives.

Professional sports people uphold important ethical values such as fairness, integrity and self-discipline. Professional sport is the focus of many people's enjoyment and aspiration and it is something that people care deeply about. Sport plays a complex role in society: it is lucrative, as well as political, historical, hierarchical and symbolic. This is landscape that today's sports graduate has to navigate. A graduate who is an independent, critical thinker, amenable to reason and willing to act is someone who is better equipped to enter this world and make an impact. The study of ethics enhances this ability to make an impact.

References

Athanassoulis, N. (2006) An Introduction to Ethical Thinking. *Resources for Teaching Inter-Disciplinary Ethics*. Leeds: IDEA CETL University of Leeds. Accessed 12.12.10 from http://www.idearesources.leeds.ac.uk/Default.aspx?Id=18)

Barnett, R. (2000) Supercomplexity and the Curriculum. *Studies in Higher Education* **25** (3) 255–65

Inter-Disciplinary Ethics Applied (IDEA) (2008–present) *Inter-Disciplinary Ethics Resources Database* Leeds: IDEA CETL University of Leeds. Accessed 12.12.10 from http://www.idearesources.leeds.ac.uk/Default.aspx?Id=20

QAA (2008) Subject benchmark statements. Accessed 08.02.11 from http://www.qaa.ac.uk/academicinfrastructure/benchmark/honours/default.asp

GRACE ROBINSON is a tutor of philosophy and applied ethics at the University of Leeds, and the project leader for the Sport Ethics Research Development Project (SERP) funded in part by the Higher Education Academy Hospitality, Leisure, Sport and Tourism (HLST) Subject Network. This project has made links between colleagues teaching sport ethics across the country and Europe; bringing together a collection of their teaching materials for publication online. Grace is also the director of an independent education practice *Thinking Space*, taking philosophical ideas into schools, community groups and businesses.

KAREN LLEWELLYN has taught sports ethics in higher education for over ten years. At the University of Leeds, she has been involved in the work of the IDEA CETL, in particular, embedding ethics in the sport and exercise sciences programme and also the development of an HLST-funded sports ethics online learning and teaching resource. She has led cross-institutional projects including the Research-Informed Teaching Project at York St John University (2006–9) and is currently completing the Leeds Building Capacity Project in Research, Learning and Teaching (2010–11).

ACKNOWLEDGEMENTS

The authors would like to acknowledge the work of Georgia Testa, Lecturer in Medical Ethics at the University of Leeds. Her work on an earlier guide to teaching applied ethics informed this chapter.

The authors also wish to thank the University of Leeds IDEA CETL staff for their support in the teaching of sports ethics which has provided the foundations to this chapter; in particular Professor Christopher Megone, centre director, Dr Jim Parry (former) assistant centre director, Kathryn Blythe, centre manager, Dr Rob Lawlor, Dr David Lewis, Dr Alice Temple and Tom Williams. In addition, thanks go to Patsy Kemp, for her support in establishing a sports ethics special interest group, a forum for the advocacy of teaching sports ethics.

6

Middlesex University Mentoring Network
Student perspectives on their learning journey and opportunities for impact

Julie Haddock-Millar, Nwamaka Onyiuke, Helen Villalobos,
Raymond Asumadu, Gifty Gabor and Tulsi Derodra
Middlesex University

This chapter reports on a recent initiative – the development
of the first Middlesex University Mentoring Network (MUMN)
– created and developed by undergraduate and postgraduate
students at Middlesex University (MU) Business School.

Introduction

The authors, three second-year undergraduate BA Human Resource Management (HRM) students, Asumadu, Gabor and Derodra, two part-time MA Human Resource Development (HRD) students, Onyiuke and Villalobos, and one professional doctoral student, Haddock-Millar, give their perspectives on their learning journey and the opportunities they have created, through the MUMN, to become and enable others to be graduates with impact.

This chapter reports on their journey during the last 12 months. The discussion draws attention to the changing profession map of the Chartered Institute of Personnel and Development (CIPD), and the influence this has had on the group's approach and practice. The group define the purpose of the MUMN, what it is designed to achieve and why. The main features of the approach are highlighted, in particular, the enablers to success. Evidence of effectiveness to-date is presented, demonstrating impact and relevance. The barriers to the development of the MUMN are explored, as are the lessons learned, which will inform others embarking on such a journey.

Context

In light of the growing concern around rising graduate unemployment (CBI, 2009: 4) and the changing CIPD map (2009a), Haddock-Millar identified an opportunity to support the career development of others, creating opportunities to enhance skills, behaviours and knowledge, enabling students and practitioners to develop their personal and professional impact in the workplace. She discussed the concept with a number of part-time postgraduate students, who were also practitioners. Two students, Onyiuke and Villalobos, offered to support the initiative and help to get the network off the ground, bringing together students, alumni, academic staff and practitioners through a formal mentoring network.

The group created the MUMN in November 2009. The development of the network coincided with research conducted by the CIPD resulting in new foundations for practice and a new HR profession map. Common to all membership levels is the behavioural concept of the thinking performer (CIPD, 2009b). The thinking performer places increased emphasis on practice, skills and behaviours, rather than on knowledge. Knowledge is still an important element of membership, as professionals need to apply knowledge to practice; however, the emphasis is also on *what* the individual does and *how* the individual does it.

Specifically, the thinking performer focuses on results and processes; reflects on the ways things are done in order to seek ways of doing them better, challenges people about the things that are currently done, understands the purpose of tasks and activities and presents an ethical attitude, articulating concerns when appropriate. The founding members felt it important to assist fellow learners to prepare for the changing demands and expectations of the profession, and in particular the increased focus on behaviours. The network's framework was the employability model developed by Frame and Haddock (2009) demonstrating the connection between the learning domains (Figure 6.1).

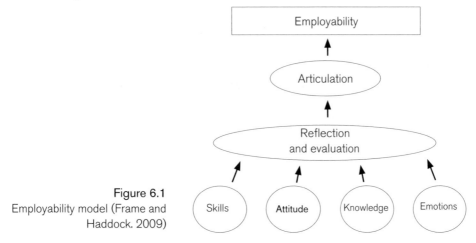

Figure 6.1
Employability model (Frame and Haddock. 2009)

The development process
The founding members agreed on a developmental process, designed as a three-step approach to maximise commitment and collaboration.

Stage 1   Engaging stakeholders
The founding team began their journey by holding a meeting with 37 first-year BA HRM students, asking the group if they would like to be involved in a mentoring

network, and if so, what they would want from this network. The discussion revealed that many students were already thinking about their long-term employability and wanted to gain a more practical understanding of the profession. It also highlighted that they would value the opportunity to build their professional networks, which they recognised would be critical to enhancing their career opportunities in a turbulent climate. Overall, this meeting demonstrated a significant interest and demand for a mentoring programme. On this basis, the team organised the first mentoring session, in which students were invited to meet possible mentors and the founding team, and discuss the approach they would like to take in building the mentoring programme.

Stage 2   Securing funding and support

The Centre of Excellence for Work Based Learning (CEWBL) at MU was offering small funding grants up to the value of £3,000, for projects designed to enhance graduate employability. The team thought this was an ideal opportunity to gain a small amount of funding to enable support for upcoming events and the development of a network website. They completed a funding application which was approved by the director of the CEWBL; at the same time, the director gave the team an opportunity to gain support for the network by sharing their vision at a variety of forums.

Stage 3   Developing opportunities

Once the team had secured the funding, they organised and participated in the following activities:

- ❏ Ten mentoring group sessions
- ❏ Presentation of the project at the European Mentoring and Coaching Council (EMCC) annual conference, 2010
- ❏ The first MUMN 2010 Annual Conference, titled *Unleashing your potential through mentoring* for 33 delegates, including students, alumni, academic staff and practitioners (see Plate 6)
- ❏ Organisation of a mentee site visit to a large charitable organisation to understand HR management in practice
- ❏ Development of the MUMN brand and logo with an external media company
- ❏ Launch of the MUMN website www.thecoachvine.com
- ❏ Link created with the International Centre for the Study of Coaching (ICSC), MU.

Discussion

This section provides individual narrative accounts from the core members of the MUMN. The focus of discussion is the impact the Network has had on their personal and professional journeys and the nature of the relationships they have developed.

Reflections on experience: individual narrative accounts

Julie Haddock-Millar

My goal is to raise the aspirations of group members, providing opportunities that might not usually arise within the context of their studies and stakeholder group, enriching their personal and professional lives. Perhaps the greatest impact has been to provide mentors and mentees with the opportunity to collaborate with external partners. One such example was when David Clutterbuck invited the core members to write a case-study book chapter in his forthcoming publication *The Diversity Mentoring Casebook*. This provided a fantastic opportunity for the group to develop their technical skills and knowledge (Brockbank and McGill, 2006: 63) specifically around research, inquiry and publishing.

This opportunity arose at the launch of the ICSC, which brought together students, practitioners and academics. At the Conference, the mentees participated in group discussions around the dynamics between practitioner and academic research within the context of learning and development in higher education, engaging in topical conversation, challenging current practice and suggesting innovative ways to engage learners. It was at this launch that Clutterbuck invited the student participants to contribute to a new case-study book featuring diversity, culture and ethnicity. As a result of this initiative, those involved will be situated in a credible position to tackle workplace challenges, drawing upon their knowledge and experience from the network.

Nwamaka Onyiuke

I work with a third sector organisation, Jesus House for All Nations, that is keen to make a difference by helping people discover purpose, maximise their potential and therefore positively impact their community. The MUMN created a great opportunity for me to get involved in an area I am passionate about and avail myself to help some committed undergraduate students discover their purpose and achieve as much as they possibly can in life. Being part of the MUMN has been a catalyst in helping me develop greater skills in the workplace, enhancing my career opportunities. My key learning point has been the appreciation of the benefits of maximising my potential, collaborating with different communities of practice, engaging with diverse groups and learning the value of networking.

As a result of my connection with Haddock-Millar through the MUMN, I recently had the pleasure of facilitating the induction programme for the business school's flagship MA in Human Resource Management/Human Resource Development. This highlights to me the importance of credibility in the workplace and in any setting; you never know how the people around you can influence your future growth. As a result of the diverse conversations that take place in our Network, we are constantly giving 360° feedback to each other, which gives greater self-awareness: I really value the feedback from my 360° workplace stakeholder group.

As a learning and development facilitator one of the challenges in the workplace is helping people to see the value of continuous personal development (CPD) and taking ownership for their CPD. This experience has broadened my learning and given me the opportunity to share the value of investing in and managing CPD with students and staff in my workplace. Working alongside stakeholders above, across and below can open doors, establish new partnerships and group collaborations, increasing the scope of opportunities.

An example of such an opportunity is the forthcoming Jesus House Leadership Impact Conference 2011. The Conference will bring together 1,000 attendees from across the globe to equip leaders to develop their people and impact their world. The MUMN members will help facilitate the event and participate in the workshops. The ultimate gain for the network members is the personal and professional workplace benefit it brings them. Indeed, Klasen and Clutterbuck (2007: 1) state that 'mentoring is one of the best methods of enhancing individuals learning and development in all works of life'.

Helen Villalobos

Participating in the Network has led to a number of personal benefits. My network has increased considerably, as I have been introduced to new communities of practice such as the ICSC, EMCC and CEWBL. As a result, the network has had a key influence in facilitating a number of new social relationships including academics and HRM practitioners, university professional services and a wider range of fellow students than I would otherwise have known. I have been able to transfer into my own academic and teaching practice what I have learned from these new learning partnerships which foster discussion, debate and reflection on new ideas across the fields of coaching and mentoring.

My mentor has been instrumental in empowering me to develop a number of key CIPD behaviours, in particular, becoming more personally credible. She provides me with feedback which increases my self-awareness, helps me to re-frame personal dilemmas and identify constructive ways of dealing with difficult situations. In turn, the opportunity to mentor others provides me with an opportunity to practise these new behaviours. Indeed, a key capability of the effective mentor is being able to adapt to a much wider range of behaviours (Clutterbuck, 2004: 4). The opportunity to mentor and be mentored simultaneously in the same space, is a uniquely enriching feature of the regular meetings. In discussions with the players (mentees) I can share insights of my own, yet also draw on the rich perspectives of more experienced participants as I grapple with my own dilemmas.

Working so closely with fellow participants has also enabled me to understand the learning challenges others experience, providing valuable insights which inform how I facilitate learning in others. I notice how my coaching capability has increased, as I have learned to draw on a wider range of reflective questions which enable me to build rapport and understand more deeply what fellow participants grapple with. It has been enriching to see the HR profession viewed through the eyes of mentees, and their questions have often prompted me to reconsider the assumptions I carry about the profession myself.

In addition, as participants reflect on how they have developed through the network, there is an enormous sense of personal satisfaction at what we have all achieved together. The future impact of this initiative outside of the network will be that the participants feel able to take on larger more complex projects, such as the Jesus House Leadership Conference, which extend our professional portfolios and have a vital impact on the communities within which we live, work and serve.

Raymond Asumadu

Involvement in the Network has helped me to become more self-aware. One of the mentoring sessions I participated in was a discussion around the concept of emotional intelligence (Goleman, 1998: 28). Understanding my emotional intelligence, recognising my own feelings and the feelings of others has helped me to build stronger relationships with my colleagues at university and in the workplace. The importance of non-verbal communication has also made me more aware of my behaviours and how I interact with others in everyday life. This could make the difference between me being employed in an organisation, or not, following the interview process.

Organising the inaugural MUMN Conference had the greatest impact on me. Exposure to the professional environment and listening to inspirational people has encouraged me to work harder to get to where I want to be, developed my self-belief and career aspirations. The opportunity to present in a formal environment at the MUMN conference also boosted my confidence in terms of the kind of presentation which will be required in the workplace.

Gifty Gabor

A mentor is someone who has the inner competence to pass on knowledge and skills through example, inner authority, and dialogue (Hudson, 1999). I have formed long-term relationships with members on the team and gained valuable knowledge from a wide range of expertise in the human resources field. I am not only part of a dynamic team; I am also being equipped to be a difference maker at my workplace by identifying opportunities to add value and tackle challenges to improve the work environment. Planning the inaugural conference was an honour, as well as developing my communication and interpersonal skills. At the conference I had the opportunity to meet many practitioners, including Clive Wilson, an inspirational coach and mentor. I was also given the opportunity to visit a large charitable organisation, Jesus House. It was a privilege to see the theory of human resource management in practice. The visit also provided an opportunity to network with people in the workplace, ask questions and think about my future career plans in light of the exposure to practice.

Tulsi Derodra

A mentor is someone who takes you under his or her wing and provides advice and guidance to help you move in the right direction. Having a mentor is the greatest gift, therefore having Julie, Helen, and Nwamaka as part of my life is indeed the greatest gift. They are very open-minded and ever ready and willing to help. When I joined the network I had no prior human resource management experience; I was given the opportunity to visit a large charitable organisation, gaining an insight into the day-to-day activities in a human resource management department. Planning a conference as part of the network created an opportunity to enhance my organisational, team working, and presentation skills as well as increasing my confidence to present in front of a large audience.

Having gained these skills and knowledge will enable me to organise other events outside university, perform in a team of co-workers and present in front of people with confidence – although a lot of practice will be required in this area. However, as the sayings go, 'practice makes perfect' and 'Rome was not built in a day.' Mentoring has provided me with the opportunity to practise, improve, and demonstrate emotional intelligence skills and capabilities which employers regard as essential for applicants to have (Colley, 2003: 21).

Challenges and lessons learned

The success of the MUMN has not been without its challenges. These included time pressure on academic staff to enable communication, scheduling group meetings and meeting with employers. Within two months of launching the programme the BA HRM Programme leader and a key supporter retired from post. The founding team had taken time to build up rapport and confidence with the programme leader, allowing the team to take up valuable class time, which was lost upon her departure. Holding network meetings proved difficult due to clashing schedules and commitments. Involving employers and securing visits proved challenging as they were reluctant to allow visitors on site. However, the team worked around class commitments, adopted a flexible approach to meeting venues and times, worked with local employers to secure access and developed a website platform to communicate with a wider network of participants.

There are a number of key lessons we take away from our participation in MUMN so far. First, the importance of continually looking to expand our professional networks and the impact this has on our long term employability. With so few jobs openly advertised in a recessionary climate, the capacity to access the 'hidden' jobs market becomes ever more critical. This can only be achieved through widening our range of contacts. With this comes the increasing confidence to reach out to new people and opportunities, and as Megginson and Whitaker (2008: 116) advise 'First, do not be afraid to ask. If you are rejected, don't worry. You are no worse off than you were before you tried.' This is an important ethos MUMN has encouraged us to adopt.

MUMN has also taught us the powerful impact that learning partnerships can have. Collaborative partnerships between academics, students and practitioners, where we come together as fellow learners, provide a rich source of new learning and can complement some of the more traditional class based approaches. In many ways MUMN has shifted away from top-down vertical learning relationships between these stakeholders, towards 'horizontal, consensual, collaborative modes of bringing people together to make something different happen' (Cleveland, 2004: 21). Examples include developing and running our first student-led conference, during which students become more accountable and empowered to lead their own learning journeys (Clutterbuck, 2004: 19). These experiences in turn provide new insights which can be applied to our academic practice and job searches, and enable us to offer something different from our peers.

Summary

The success of the MUMN is largely due to its organic nature, evolving over a period of twelve months, transitioning from a small group of students meeting on an informal basis, to a professional network which has a group identity, logo and web-based platform (www.thecoachvine.com).

Figure 6.2
The Middlesex University Mentoring Network Logo

The network has 20 connected members, with an equal balance of students and practitioners. The next 12 months (December 2010 to December 2011) will involve growing the network, assisting in the development of three events with the ICSC, MU and opening out the programme to all undergraduate and postgraduate students in the business school.

The MUMN has already made a substantial impact on those involved evidenced by the core members' narrative accounts of their learning journey. The experience of those involved in the network will enable them to have impact in the world of work. This will be evidenced by their influence, contribution and the results they achieve. Based on the MUMN model, members will be equipped to influence others to identify low cost, high impact innovative solutions to address organisational challenges.

As a direct result of their involvement in the network, Onyiuke and Villalobos now teach on a part-time basis within the business school. Their contribution is evidenced by their engagement with student cohorts, drawing upon stories from their student, practitioner and teaching experience. In particular, they encourage learners to critically evaluate the theory within the context of the organisational environment. In order to achieve the best results, organisations need to bring together fragmented departments and eliminate silos. The members will be able to draw on their experience of connecting geographically, culturally and ethnically diverse people to work towards a common purpose. The Network will continue to have impact in the future, primarily because the group members are committed to the growth and development of each other, the Network and the community, aspiring to maximize each other's potential.

References

Brockbank, A. and McGill, I. (2006) *Facilitating Reflective Learning Through Mentoring and Coaching*. London: Kogan Page Limited

CIPD (2009a) Map available at: http://www.cipd.co.uk/hr-profession-map/faqs.htm#q4 Accessed 05/02/2011

CIPD (2009b) Available at http://www.cipd.co.uk/about/profstands/thinkingperformer.htm. Accessed on 05/12/2010

Confederation of British Industry, (2009) *Employment Trends, Work patterns in the Recession.* (online) Available at: http://www.cbi.org.uk/ndbs/press Accessed on 05/12/2010

Cleveland, H. (2004) Leading and learning with nobody in charge. In Connor, M. and Clawson, J. (2004) (eds) *Creating a learning culture – strategy, technology and practice*. Cambridge University Press

Clutterbuck, D. (2004) *Everyone needs a mentor – Fostering talent in your organisation*. 4th ed. London: Chartered Institute of Personnel and Development

Colley, H. (2003) Mentoring for Social Inclusion. A critical approach to nurturing mentor relationships. Routledge

Frame, P. and Haddock, J. (2009) What can MYSAKE do to support enhancing personal development planning and employability. Work Based Learning Futures III Conference, April 23–24. University of Derby

Goleman, D. (1998) *Working with Emotional Intelligence*. New York: Bantam Books

Hudson, F. M. (1999) *The Handbook of Coaching*. San Francisco: Jossey Bass

Klasen, N. and Clutterbuck, D. (2007) *Implementing Mentoring Schemes*. Oxford: Elsevier

Megginson, D and Whitaker, V (2008) *Continuing professional development*. London: Chartered Institute of Personnel and Development

MUMN (2010) www.thecoachvine.com

JULIE HADDOCK-MILLAR is a lecturer in the Human Resource Management Department, Middlesex University Business School. She is currently completing her professional doctorate, focusing on strategic organisational development with Middlesex University. Her main areas of research are green human resource development, organisational change, learning and development.

NWAMAKA ONYIUKE is a learning and development consultant, qualified life coach and mentor. She works with Jesus House, London. She is currently completing her MA in human resource development with Middlesex University. Her passion is helping others to maximise their potential, supporting their learning and development.

HELEN VILLALOBOS is a freelance learning and development facilitator and lecturer in the Human Resource Management Department, Middlesex University Business School. She is currently completing her MA in Human Resource Development with Middlesex University. Her research interests include continuing professional development, individual and organisational change.

RAYMOND ASUMADU is a second-year BA HRM student at Middlesex University and student representative. His passion is learning and development, he joined the network to develop his skills in order to become an all round professional. His career interests are recruitment and selection, training and career development.

GIFTY GABOR is a second-year BA HRM student at Middlesex University and student representative. She works on a part-time basis in customer service. Her passion is to end her day knowing she has had a great impact in someone's life. Her career aspiration is to open a training and development centre for charitable organisations in Ghana.

TULSI DERODRA is a second-year BA HRM student at Middlesex University. She works on a part-time basis as a healthcare advisor. Her passion is learning and development, she joined the network to gain knowledge and develop her network of professional contacts.

7

Embedding graduate skills

Leigh Wood *Macquarie University*
and
Anne Daly *University of Canberra*

This chapter presents strategies to implement graduate skills
in business undergraduate programmes.[1] We have developed
teaching and learning resources to cultivate and grade student
learning in the four areas of teamwork, critical thinking, ethical
practice and sustainability.[2] We discuss our experience
of implementing resources at a programme level, and in a
discrete, intensive workshop for high-achieving students.

Context

Australia has 38 universities offering business undergraduate programmes. The
Australian Learning and Teaching Council (ALTC) funds projects to support learning
and teaching at Australian universities and the Australian Business Deans Council
(ABDC) supports learning and teaching in business faculties. There are around
173,000 full-time equivalent students studying business-related degrees in Australia.

Our *Graduate Skills* project arose from the concerns of industry about graduates' preparedness for work. A scoping study of industry representatives in Australia
(Freeman et al, 2008) indicated a widespread industry belief that the attainment of
graduate skills is one of the key areas in which graduates are underperforming, even
though all Australian universities have graduate/generic skills/attributes/capabilities
listed in their policy statements. There was clearly a need to address the learning
and assessment of these capabilities in discipline-specific contexts. For our project,
which was funded by the ALTC and supported by the ABDC, we selected three of the
capabilities (teamwork, critical thinking, ethical practice) that were identified in the
scoping study and added sustainability as an emerging graduate capability required
by business.

---

1   This chapter presents a component of the project on behalf of the project team: Marilyn Clark-
     Murphy (Edith Cowan University), Theda Thoma (Australian Catholic University), Lynne
     Leveson (La Trobe University), Peter Dixon (University of Tasmania), Peter Petocz (Macquarie
     University), Marie Kavanagh (Southern Queensland University), Brendan Rigby and Tori Vu
     (project managers).
2   These materials were tested and refined with students and academics through multiple
     iterations, and can be used, adapted and embedded in an undergraduate business programme
     and they are available on the Graduate Skills website (www.graduateskills.edu.au).

This project has demonstrated that a workshop model can effectively address the development of graduate capabilities, and has made available a range of teaching materials that can be used to help students engage with these capabilities and to assess the extent of their learning. Importantly, the project has investigated the development of these capabilities in a holistic way, rather than as isolated skills. Including ethical practice and sustainability has shown that the approach can be applied to dispositional development in addition to the learning of more clearly-defined skills such as teamwork and critical thinking.

Rationale

We use the term 'graduate skills' to refer to the skills, attributes and capabilities demonstrated by graduates on completing an undergraduate degree. We will not discuss the body of research in this area and refer you to a literature review at our website (Rigby et al, 2009).

We report on practical strategies to foster business graduate skills. The resources include a wide range of targeted activities, from research to teaching activities, such as:

❏ real-world case studies and supplementary reading material
❏ suggested teaching methods and lesson plans
❏ literature reviews identifying best practice
❏ standards of achievement, providing a framework to assess the attainment of each skill
❏ guidelines for using the resources.

Many of the project learning and teaching resources are being used in undergraduate and postgraduate business, statistics and interdisciplinary units in the seven participating institutions, some as a trial initiative and others on a more permanent basis.

The following section describes the resources and rubrics we developed. We then discuss two examples: our experience of implementing programme level standards at the University of Tasmania, and an intensive workshop for high-achieving students at Macquarie University.

Learning and teaching graduate skills

We identified the following best practice principles in teaching graduate skills (Bowden et al, 2000):

❏ The development of graduate skills is best fostered in the context of disciplinary learning. That is, in the discipline of business, more attention needs to be paid to how graduate skills are acquired and developed, and to the role of teaching and learning strategies in promoting and enhancing these skills.
❏ A learner-centred approach, located in constructivist pedagogy, is considered best practice as it situates the experiences, goals, and values of the students at the centre of the learning process, therefore enhancing their cognitive and

affective development.

❏ It is essential to adopt an approach to teaching and learning that allows teachers to focus simultaneously on the students' self-regulation of the learning and motivation processes, as well as on the environmental triggers that affect these processes.

The lesson plan for a learning activity focusing on sustainability (the Gunns Mill scenario, Appendix A) is presented as an example of the resources we developed, tested and implemented. The activity relates to the proposed development of a paper mill in Tasmania, but the principles involved are applicable to any development proposal that is likely to have environmental effects. Accompanying the lesson plan for the case study are a number of resources including general information about the scenario, as well as expositions of the perspectives of the most prominent stakeholders. It is built on these best-practice principles:

❏ Clear learning outcomes, which allow for constructive alignment and effective and targeted assessment (Treleaven & Voola, 2008).

❏ Allowing students to engage critically with the concept, policy and practice of sustainability in the business environment rather than prescribing a definition of sustainability. Students learn to understand and think about different perspectives of sustainability through a stakeholder analysis. This builds on existing research into education for sustainability.

❏ The idea of 'jigsaw groups'. These allow students to become 'experts' in a particular supporting document or materials for the activity, and then to share that knowledge with other students. This is an example of good practice in collaborative learning, where students teach and learn from one another (see Macquarie, 2010).

❏ Building on and developing students' self-regulated learning by facilitating both interpersonal and internal learning opportunities. Students work in their group to reach consensus, then reflect on how those decision-making processes were developed.

The resources can act as templates for the design of other activities to promote and enhance a variety of graduate skills across the business curriculum. Our materials include:

❏ other real-world case studies, such as one on drug testing and another on the Moreton Bay, Queensland oil spill
❏ the argumentative essay
❏ icebreakers
❏ debates
❏ the jigsaw method
❏ ethical dilemma scenarios.

An important aspect of the development of these resources was their evaluation by students and teachers, using both qualitative and quantitative measures.

Assessing graduate skills

Another major feature of the Graduate Skills project was the development and testing of standards of achievement. We considered it crucial that standards of achievement were displayed, for university grading purposes as well as for students' benefit in terms of their learning outcomes.

We developed rubrics to demonstrate students' attainment of each of the graduate skills. The rubric for critical thinking is set out as an example of the skill and discipline-specific assessment framework (see Appendix B). We also developed a generic rubric, which allows teachers, faculties and institutions to adapt it for their own assessment purposes across discipline and skill domains. These models, as well as those rubrics for teamwork, ethical practice and sustainability are also available on the Graduate Skills website.

The rubrics define five levels of understanding based on qualitatively different outcomes from student engagement with materials throughout the project. There is a clear connection with the levels of the SOLO taxonomy (Biggs & Collis, 1982). The levels also correspond easily with the typical grading in Australia of high distinction (HD), distinction (D), credit (C), pass (P) and fail (F). The articulation of these rubrics – in particular, the verbs that express how students are expected to learn and demonstrate achievement – allow constructive alignment with learning outcomes and learning activities. The rubrics enable students and academics to express, measure and demonstrate achievement and learning against cognitive domains. They set out what students are expected to achieve alongside what they have and have not achieved; this approach allows appropriate feedback to be given to students, and serves as a reference for quality assurance.

The standards of achievement are defined in relation to three different domains of knowledge: conceptual, procedural and professional. This allows teachers to design learning and assessment tasks that give students the opportunity to demonstrate their conceptual understanding of the capability, the procedures to carry out the graduate skill, and also to show their professional application of the skill's principles and practices. The standards are focused at the graduate level, so more students would be expected to demonstrate higher levels in later-year assessments: however, first-year students can demonstrate a similar range of achievements, though perhaps with more structured tasks. The standards include guidance on creating criteria and levels of achievement to suit the particular task being assessed as well as the appropriate level for students.

Examples

Redesigning the curriculum: University of Tasmania

The resources and insights of the projects have had an impact at a programme level at the University of Tasmania. In the Faculty of Business, the Bachelor of Business programme was substantially reviewed during 2009 to comply with the university's common course structure. In concert with this, the Faculty of Business engaged in mapping graduate attributes across major strands of study. From 2011, a new compulsory core unit in the Bachelor of Business Programme will cover teamwork and critical thinking.

The unit co-ordinator will use of some of the resources and assessment rubrics developed by the project with embedding of teamwork and critical thinking in major strands of study at an intermediate and advanced level. The project's activities and outcomes have been particularly influential in informing these processes. At a unit level, the ethical dilemma scenarios have been considered for use in a capstone *Ethics* unit. The jigsaw method of student engagement has been used in a second-year *Industrial Relations* unit.

In this model of teaching graduate skills in separate, dedicated units of study but applied or 'infused' in units across the curriculum, the advantage is that teaching of the skills is done by people who specialise in the area. The disadvantage is that staff training is needed, so that they know what has been taught before and understand that they have a responsibility to develop and assess these skills in their units. A clear map and audit of the development of the skills and where they are taught and assessed in the curriculum is in the process of being developed.

Workshop for high-achieving students: Macquarie University

Throughout the project, 80 academics and 81 students drawn from a mix of business discipline areas from twenty Australian universities participated in a series of workshops facilitated by the team. These workshops were used by the team to trial and refine learning modules and rubrics, and to facilitate professional development for staff. They also enabled the development of a workshop model for teaching graduate skills. A key principle underpinning the concept of embedding is that it is not simply a process of information transfer but involves a degree of transformation in the way that graduate skills are conceived and applied to relevant situations; for example, through case studies, problem solving, debates and class discussion. An effective feature of the workshops has been the high quality of the face-to-face interaction between students, teachers and resource materials.

As a direct outcome of the project, this model was implemented in the form of an intensive workshop programme to enhance the graduate skills of high-achieving students at Macquarie University. This programme will service students who have received a high university entrance score ('merit scholars'), and it will include an average of 40 scholars each year, the majority from business, and the remainder from the merit scholars programme.

The first merit scholar workshop was held as a residential over three days, and included later-year business students from a number of Australian universities. After initial icebreaker exercises, they worked in groups on a variety of exercises and activities that focused on increasing their awareness and proficiency in dealing with the four targeted graduate skills, as developed in the project. These activities were led by academics and educational developers, from a range of disciplines, who provided feedback to students on their participation and their reflection on practice and application. The three-day event culminated in a series of group presentations in which each group received feedback from other students, staff and visiting industry liaison representatives.

The workshop model was found to be an effective teaching method, because it gave a sustained block of time which could be used to cover a range of important graduate skills, and provided the opportunity to focus on particular exercises. The workshop attested to the efficacy of social interaction as a means of improving students' understanding of these capabilities. Student participants responded enthusiastically to the workshops. Successful uptake of graduate skills at the undergraduate level relies not just on academic staff developing and adhering to learning and teaching policy and procedure, but also student buy-in of the value of graduate skills.

Student quotes from the workshops

At the end of the workshops students were invited to provide written feedback and some were also interviewed. Twenty-one students were contacted six months after the first workshop and interviewed. The student comments about the workshop experience (some of which are included here) were overwhelmingly positive and related to the following themes in their learning; academic benefits, personal development, the social context of learning, transferability to employment and transferability to other cultural settings.

> I loved the workshop. ... I learned a lot from it. I pushed myself. All these great experiences add up a lot ... I just want to reiterate that I am encouraged by the fact that you guys are doing something like this, and I really hope that it will come to something and it will impact the way that the university teaches, and hopefully improve its standards as well.

> Because I think where we learn in China, the majority is based on – you know we don't have a lot of workshops ... we have lectures so it's different. Nothing involves a lot of activities. So I think if you involve a lot of activities and students participate in what's going on and contribute to the workshop, that's a very good way of learning.

Main learning points
Workshops as professional development

While we designed workshops to test and develop resources and rubrics, they surprisingly provided a transformational model for professional development. Seeing academics and students working with interactive materials made a significant impression on staff who observed it, and this has resulted in many using the resources in their own classes. The workshop programme is an effective ongoing professional development initiative to equip academics in embedding graduate skills into their own teaching.

Workshops as capstone experiences

Workshops are resource intensive; more difficult with larger groups; and they require special timing in the academic year. These represent very real constraints. However, through experience, observation and analysis of feedback from students and academics, the project team was able to identify a range of areas in teaching and learning where this model of delivery was considered to be particularly effective, for example, in a capstone unit.

Rubrics

The development and testing of rubrics with students resulted in more robust rubrics that genuinely differentiated between qualitatively different attainments which could be translated into a rubric for use in designing, assessing and communication requirements of learning tasks.

In summary, the development of graduate skills has now been widely recognised as important in business degrees. The workshop model complements other models based on the embedded, infused or dedicated approaches used to develop these skills among students. Workshops can be used to kick-start learning at the beginning of a degree or to consolidate learning in capstone units.

Conclusion

Transitions to and from university learning are critical parts of a journey to becoming a professional (Wood & Solomonides, 2008). Our project worked with students and academics to develop robust materials and techniques for embedding graduate skills. The influence on the participants was clear and demonstrated in interviews six months after the intervention workshop. It was clear from students' responses that our project had identified the skills and strategies which would enable them, as graduates, to adapt in rapidly changing environments and to be effective in their professional lives and as engaged citizens.

Whether the same results are scalable to the numbers of students studying business remains to be seen; however, the project has demonstrated that short, intensive interventions are effective. Industry panellists were impressed with the standard of student presentations and all the materials have been endorsed by our industry reference group. While studying for a degree, students should have the opportunity for a transformational learning experience and we have found that targeted materials and inspirational teaching can make an impact.

References

Biggs, J. B. & Collis, K. F. (1982) *Evaluating the Quality of Learning: the SOLO taxonomy.* Academic Press: New York

Bowden, J., Hart, G., King, B., Trigwell, K. & Watts, O., (2000), *Generic capabilities of ATN university graduates*. Accessed 1st April 2009 from http://www.clt.uts.edu.au/ATN.grad.cap.project.index.html

Freeman, M., Hancock, P., Simpson, L., Sykes, C., Petocz, P., Densten, I. & Gibson, K. (2008) *Business as Usual: A collaborative and inclusive investigation of the existing resources, strengths, gaps and challenges to be addressed for sustainability in teaching and learning in Australian university business faculties*. Scoping Report. Australian Business Deans Council

Graduate Skills (2010) *Gunns Mill Scenario* http://www.graduateskills.edu.au/wp-content/uploads/2010/08/Sustainability-and-Teamwork_Gunns-Mill.pdf.

Macquarie (2010) A booklet on leading discussions at http://www.mq.edu.au/ltc/resources/FBE_resources.htm

Rigby, B., Wood, L., Clark-Murphy, M., Daly, A., Dixon, P., Kavanagh, M., Leveson, L., Petocz, P. & Thomas, T. (2009), *Review of Graduate Skills: Critical Thinking, Teamwork, Ethical Practice and Sustainability*. Accessed 11 August, 2010 from http://www.graduateskills.edu.au/literature-review

Treleaven, L. & Voola, R., (2008) Integrating the development of graduate attributes through constructive alignment. *Journal of Marketing Education* 20 160–73

Wood, L. N. & Solomonides, I. (2008) Different disciplines, different transitions. *Mathematics Education Research Journal* 20 (2) 117–34

LEIGH WOOD is the associate dean, learning and teaching, Faculty of Business and Economics, Macquarie University. She has a strong record of research in learning and teaching with over 30 journal articles, three textbooks, 10 multimedia learning packages and is the co-editor of the 'How to …' series available at http://www.mq.edu.au/ltc/resources/FBE_resources.htm. Recently she has coordinated a curriculum review of the undergraduate and postgraduate degrees in business at Macquarie University. She is currently writing a book on transition to professional work.

ANNE DALY is currently the director of graduate studies in the Faculty of Business and Government at the University of Canberra with overall responsibility for the masters coursework programmes and the higher degree by research students. Her research interests are in labour economics, particularly the economic status of women and indigenous Australians. She is a member of a team working on a two-year ALTC project Internationalisation at Home. The project involves the business and health faculties at the University of Canberra and Griffith University.

ACKNOWLEDGEMENTS

The authors would like to thank Marilyn Clark-Murphy (recently retired as Professor of Finance, Edith Cowan University) Theda Thomas (Associate Dean, Learning and Teaching Australian Catholic University) Lynne Leveson (Director of Teaching and Learning, School of Management, La Trobe University) Peter Dixon (Associate Dean, Learning and Teaching, Faculty of Business and Law, University of Tasmania) Peter Petocz (Department of Statistics Macquarie University) Marie Kavanagh (professor of accounting University of Southern Queensland) and Brendan Rigby (Macquarie University)

Support for this project has been provided by the Australian Learning and Teaching Council, an initiative of the Australian Government Department of Education, Employment and Workplace Relations. The views expressed in this report do not necessarily reflect the views of the Australian Learning and Teaching Council Ltd.

Appendix A   Gunns Mill case study

Sustainability and teamwork: Gunns Mill scenario

GRADUATE SKILLS

Description	Case Study Analysis
Task type	In-class or tutorial activity
Time	50 minutes
Level	Advanced
Class size	Up to 35 students
Learning outcomes	Student should be able to:
	¶ Demonstrate an understanding of sustainability in three dimensions: environmental (green; organisational [long term]); responsibility for present and future generations
	¶ Develop an argument and counterargument in two contexts
Method	Choose a case example of an organisational activity that raises sustainability issues ('the Project')
	Prepare a general factual introduction and up to five statements of the viewpoints of stakeholders.
Concluding activity	Link this back to learning about sustainability from the student activity. Issues to address might be:
	¶ What do we mean by sustainability?
	¶ How do stakeholders view sustainability differently?
Tips	Keeping time is key to the success of this activity

Student instructions

You will work in groups of five. Everyone will be given some background material on the Project. Each group will then be given some material relating to five stakeholders with differing views about the Project. One group member will be assigned to each stakeholder. You should read the material for the stakeholder you've been assigned to but don't discuss it with the rest of your group.

The groups will then be rearranged so that those with the same information become an expert group on each stakeholder's views. Each of these expert groups will consider the information given and decide how each member will present their views to 'non experts'. For example, if you're part of the organisation's stakeholder group how could you best explain the company's position to other stakeholders?

The original groups will then reconvene and will contain an expert on each stakeholder's views.

You will then consider and discuss the issues based on the background information you've been given, and the contributions of each expert who will argue the interests of their respective stakeholder.

Your discussion should include, but need not be limited to the following:

¶   What sustainability issues does the Project raise?

¶   How would the stakeholder you are representing argue the sustainability case?

¶   Based on your view of sustainability should the Project proceed?

¶   Assume the Project is going ahead; what concessions or assurances would the stakeholder you represent seek in order to feel satisfied that the project was sustainable?

You will have about 25 minutes to work on this: 10 minutes for each expert group, and then 15 minutes for the original groups.

At the end of this time each original group must give a 5 minute group presentation which addresses the following questions:

¶   What sustainability issues are relevant to the Project?

¶   Did you reach a consensus?

¶   How did your group arrive at a consensus?

¶   What conclusion did you reach as to whether this Project can proceed in a sustainable way?

Appendix B   Critical thinking, Standards of achievement

	Conceptual	Procedural	Professional
Level 4 **HD**	As the theorising and assessment of information, ideas, materials using various modes of thinking for effective interpretation. As the articulation of an argument to support a particular perspective and its justification of one or more conclusions drawn.	Thinks open-mindedly about a situation, recognising and assessing their assumptions, implications, and practical consequences in coming up with alternative solutions. Gathers and assesses relevant information, using abstract ideas to interpret the given materials effectively.	Is able to synthesise, analyse and evaluate a variety of viewpoints of a complex situation and articulate clearly well-reasoned solutions and conclusions.
Level 3 **D**	Conceptualises critical thinking as a self-monitoring and self-correcting process; discernment which can also be applied to work produced by their peers. As the consideration of various perspectives to formulate clear, concise arguments.	Can synthesise, analyse and evaluate the quality of information and connections in an applied situation, recognising inconsistencies, gaps in logic and unexplored ideas, including their own and others. Can form good, clear arguments that include various perspectives.	Comes to well-reasoned conclusions and solutions about a professional situation, testing them against relevant criteria and standards.
Level 2 **C**	Comprehends critical thinking as the ability to discern patterns and relationships between concepts. Understands the application of basic critical thinking concepts such as a reasoned argument. Understands critical thinking as the selection, collection, analysis, interpretation and evaluation of source materials.	Can use different critical thinking skills appropriately in a variety of contexts, such as making a reasoned argument or describe patterns and relationships between concepts.	Able to investigate a professional situation and determine facts and fallacies appropriate to the situation.
Level 1 **P**	Defines thinking as one or more of its basic manifestations like logic, types of argument, bias and laws.	Can apply logical thinking (inference and deduction) to simple logic exercises. Is able to take simple arguments and deconstruct them to determine the conclusion and the evidence that supports that conclusion.	Demonstrates a basic understanding of logic and analysis of argument but has little understanding of how to apply these in professional situations.
Level 0 **F**	Defines critical thinking as memorisation and/or the acceptance of information without filtering. Finds sources only to confirm their own point of view.	Unable to express themselves in a logical manner. Unable to analyse an argument or make a valid argument; accepting information at face value.	Unable to apply critical thinking tools to professional situations.

8

Enhancing graduate impact
in *Tourism Marketing Practice*

Steve Jones and Greig Headley
Leeds Metropolitan University

This chapter explores the use of a structured assessment practice to bridge the gap between the learning experienced by students on the BA (Hons) International Tourism Management degree at Leeds Metropolitan University and their mobilisation of that learning when entering the workplace. The enhancement of graduate impact over and above that prompted by a typical vocational degree is seen to give these students a unique emotional benefit in the eyes of industrial recruiters (Aaker, 1996).

Introduction

Five years ago during a programme review, the module team recognised that there is a weakness in this type of degree, which purports to be vocational. While students are armed with wide academic theory in the subject, they have little experience and awareness of how to apply this knowledge in industry working practices. The team considered that their impact as graduates would be compromised.

Tourism Marketing Practice is a final year undergraduate (Level 6) module that uses a structured assessment scenario to bridge the gap between the learning encountered by students in modules on BA (Hons) International Tourism Management and their mobilisation of that learning when entering the workplace. The assessment portfolio provides the student with real life proof of their capabilities in the marketing arena.

Objectives

Identifying the gap led the teaching team to develop a new final-year undergraduate module, *Tourism Marketing Practice*. They wanted to make their graduates more employable by creating a module which integrated academic knowledge with the skills needed to take that knowledge and implement it in the workplace. At the same time, the teaching team recognised that to achieve the desired outcomes they would have to re-think some of the more traditional teaching practices, and the types of assessment that had gone alongside this type of teaching. They believed that the learning acquired from this new approach would both support real-life situations and shorten the learning curve in those situations, by imparting essential skills to make the student a more effective manager.

Rationale

The following principles were agreed as underpinning the module design:

1 The students need to understand the relevance of the learning, teaching and assessment methods to both their studies and their future employment.
2 The experience should be enjoyable and enable students to differentiate themselves in the job market and during initial career development.
3 Students should feel pride in their achievement, empowered by their module experience, carry this through to interviews, and have impact in their work.
4 Student learning from this new approach must support real life situations, making the student a more effective future manager by giving them essential skills and a shortened learning curve in the work environment.
5 The assessment created would drive all learning and be the key to the module's success and to developing the students' employability.

The assessment rationale

The authors consider that the assessment is key to the module design. A number of practitioners have proposed that assessment is a major factor in student learning (Pickford and Brown, 2006; Race and Pickford, 2007). The Re-engineering Assessment Practices project (REAP, 2007) is a useful yardstick in measuring the success of the initial development of the module and has been a helpful set of principles for later development of the assessment and of the module as a whole. REAP lists twelve principles that the module development tried to encompass. A smaller number are relevant to this case study and covered in the discussion.

Context

The module, which is positioned as a final-year undergraduate options module, was originally designed to be part of a suite of modules contributing to a BA in Tourism Marketing Management. This degree was seen to have a strong vocational focus containing some modules specifically designed not just to impart vocational knowledge, but also to arm the students with specific work skills. This would prepare them to make an immediate contribution to an employers' organisation without having to make the leap from abstract vocational knowledge to application of this in the workplace.

The module was originally designed for 30 students but now has to be regularly capped at 45. We use IT laboratories and team teaching, with two lecturers covering different areas of expertise, but with crossover knowledge and skills, 'pushed' by student demand. The focus of the module is supported by students who recognise its relevance to their own futures and hence award it the highest student satisfaction outcomes in module surveys.

While the majority of the 'carrier' degree is guided by professional influences, this module floats working practices on these influences and requirements, enabling the development of students with real 'added value' to organisations. This is not just 'Day One' value, but value which only becomes apparent upon exposure to a work situation; it can be useful in that it can highlight areas for development in the workplace.

The module also has engaged the lecturers in new learning, especially in the cross-cultural area, where student contributions to such areas as consumer behaviour have brought new directions both to the module and to the final assessment portfolio. The module has hosted overseas students from many countries including Scandinavia, Germany, Albania, China, Japan, Hong Kong, Africa, Russia, France and Holland. This, coupled with the way students are encouraged to interact, share cultural influences and learning, truly enhances the international aspect of the degree.

Description

An essential element in the module's success has been the central role of the assessment. Here is the brief given to the students:

The Assessment

You are the new marketing manager for a small specialist tour operator who is moving into a completely new area of tours. You can choose from one of the following prospective holiday areas: adventure, religious and sacred tours, educational holidays, holidays for the over 60s, road trips, overseas city breaks.

Since these tours are an innovation, the managing director of the company has asked you to produce a sample portfolio of the materials for use in the marketing of these new tours.

You are required to individually design and justify a campaign for one of the above areas to illustrate ways the holiday product could be marketed. The campaign could include some of the following communications methods:

- direct mail (envelope and insert)
- double-page spread in a brochure
- e-mail
- design an exhibition stand (A3 working design)
- advert for a magazine (1/4 page)

and must include

- storyboard for a TV ad and/or a radio advertisement (30 seconds)
- a press release.

Your portfolio of the campaign will consist of six components. This cannot be based on any existing business.

Student centred and inclusive

While the module delivery involves team teaching, it is important to note that every student is treated as an individual and encouraged to focus on the assessment and module outputs that will encourage success in the assessment. This success will help to embed long-term 'useful' learning and add value to each student's employability.

Importantly, students have a tremendous freedom to take any direction that interests them. They can choose whatever scenario suits them within the portfolio of work and based on their future career aspirations. Little is predetermined so they are forced to make and justify decisions. The scenario, and their interpretation of it, drives everything. Classes are a mixture of core content and tutor reaction to the students' needs. The resulting class and outputs are fun, energising to teach, and a pleasure to mark.

Evaluation

The module is successful in more than one area:

❑ Because of the student enjoyment and engagement with the module, and the ensuing increased effort, the average student marks for the module are higher than in other modules, affecting the student average grades and final degree classification. The marks in the module over the past five years range from 94% – 20% with a mean of 64%.

❑ The portfolios serve as an *aide-memoire* for graduates' early working lives.

❑ The student's ability to perform, improved via engagement and relevance in the assessment, has a positive effect on the student's self esteem and confidence, both in other academic areas and in a competitive job market.

❑ Most years at least one student gets a job because of their portfolio and many students take the portfolio to interviews. (See figures 8.1–4 below).

❑ Engagement in the module in terms of commitment and student work levels. Attendance is higher than on many other final year undergraduate modules. Students encourage each other by informal continuous peer review and feedback on work developed throughout the semester and brought to class.

The module allows students to express themselves in their assessment. The key to success is the justification of all aspects of the work; not solely with the tutor in mind, but for the imaginary scenario the student creates. Students develop and critically justify their work; this skill can be carried forward into employment. An example of this commitment to a project can be seen on the right – the student is interested in working for Virgin Galactic and so created the concept 'Spa in Space' to better understand some of the issues.

Figure 8.1 An example portfolio, Spa in Space

Student comment

I really appreciated the predominantly creative part of this module. I had the freedom to do something in my field of interest, creative and practical – all in one.

Due to the way the task was set, the students were allowed to invent a tour in the field of their personal preference which was really a motivation driver. It was fun to see how the project developed and to try and produce different tools. I think this process was a helpful 'learning by doing' experience.

Moreover, by doing this project, visible and tangible results (i.e. the respective promotional tools) were produced which can be used as evidence/performance records for future job applications in the industry.

Students' best practice work is kept to be used as exemplars for the next year's

students. An exemplar can be seen in figure 8.2 (Little Chefs). Students are encouraged to share learning resources they have discovered through the virtual learning environment (VLE) for their current year and for future classes.

Figure 8.2 Little Chefs

Student comment

I really enjoyed this module and here are a few reasons why:

- The practical element made the module interesting and interactive.
- The module seemed to have a purpose, whereas a lot of other modules don't, e.g. industry usefulness for future employment.
- I enjoyed having the flexibility to choose my own project, brand and marketing material.
- The literature on x-stream (the Leeds Met VLE) was extremely useful.
- Workshops were informal yet productive.

Students engage in a creative process to address real life employment problems. They

are allowed creative freedom within the limits of their ability to justify their approach for their chosen market. With the approach shown in figures 8.3 and 8.4, the student's justification of a creative solution scored well.

Figure 8.3 V DUB holidays T shirt

Figure 8.4 V-DUB holidays paper products

Student comment

> Just wanted to say I really enjoyed this module as it gave me the chance to be creative
> and also made me realise that I would like to pursue a career in marketing.

Lecturers respond to individual student needs and aspirations. The supply of lecturers with complementary skills and the same student-centred approach is critical to the successful delivery of this teaching method.

Discussion

The evaluation above highlights the module's successes in developing employability and graduate impact. What enabled it to work? A starting point was taking a long reflective look at existing provision and the wants and needs of the students, alongside conversations with alumni about their post-graduation work experiences.

The original principles for this module's development also proved to be appropriate. It is worthwhile considering how these principles contributed to the development of graduates with impact.

The students need to understand the relevance of the learning, teaching and assessment methods to both their studies and their future employment.

As noted in the evaluation and in student feedback, the students really appreciated this. They could see that the portfolio could be used in interviews to demonstrate their capabilities. We know that a number do this every year and have had success. Students could also recognise that these were practical approaches that would be useful once in a job. Feedback from alumni is that this is indeed the case and has allowed some to have an impact early in their career.

The experience should be enjoyable and enable students to differentiate themselves in the job market and during initial career development.

The comments in the evaluation demonstrate what an enjoyable experience the students had, and indeed from the tutor's point of view, this module was a pleasure to teach. Feedback from several graduates has been that they took the portfolio to interview and it was a contributory factor in their success. We also know that this practically focused experience has been helpful to individuals creating a 'fast start' in their new post and getting them recognised in the workplace.

Student comment:

> I started my own business. Expansion has been rapid and my business is well known in my local area. One of the key factors in this has been having the know-how to produce practical and effective marketing materials. The *Tourism Marketing Practice* module really helped me in this area and gave me confidence in the approaches I adopted.

Students should feel pride in their achievement, empowered by their module experience, carry this through to interviews, and have impact in their work.

A first point for many was the achievement of producing a professional-standard portfolio. The second was often in achieving a grade that was higher by about 10% than the average they reached in other modules. This gave the students a feeling of pride in their achievement and was something taken to interview. A recent graduate noted how this had given her confidence in her first tourism marketing post.

Student learning from this new approach must support real-life situations making the student a more effective future manager, giving them essential skills and a shortened learning curve in the workplace.

This approach was developed from the industrial experience of tutors and the sorts of tasks recent graduates had been asked to perform in the workplace. We tried to develop a workshop culture that was much nearer that of a buzzing marketing department than a typical classroom. In itself, this had some unforeseen outcomes – students often stayed on at the end of sessions rather than leaving straightaway. As well as developing skills, it gave the students self-confidence.

Create an assessment that drives all learning and is the key to the module's success and developing the students' employability.

For this part of the discussion, it was decided to see how the work fitted with some of the relevant REAP principles. These are covered in the following points:

Help clarify what good performance is (goals, criteria, and standards).

This was developed as a key principle of the module but with two objectives. First, that the student had a clear idea of what was required to pass the module. This year's students have access to previous work and commentaries. Secondly, the student is made aware of what good practice in the workplace is. It was a key point for the team that the student should look at good industry practice if they were to have an impact as a graduate.

Encourage 'time and effort' on challenging learning tasks.

Motivation to put in time and effort is developed through the engagement in tasks and a realistic assessment scenario that students consider will enhance their employability and graduate skill set.

Deliver high quality feedback information that helps learners self-correct.

The students brought the assessment to every session. This allowed them to benchmark against their peers and exemplars from industry chosen by the tutors and students and to act on this feedback. Encouraging dialogue and action on feedback was seen as an essential part of developing graduate impact.

Facilitate the development of self-assessment and reflection in learning.
One aspect of having a more 'work-like' than 'classroom-like' session was that it gave the students the chance to develop self-assessment skills on a regular basis, rather than as in some modules, a one-off chance sometimes timetabled into the schemes of work. Self-assessment capability was something the module team wanted to develop in future graduates.

Support the development of learning communities
The spectre of plagiarism and collusion raises itself in many assessments in higher education. This could be due to students working on the same assessment. With this assessment, each assignment submitted is different, but it does allow the module team to foster learning communities. Working and learning in teams is often written out of module assessments, but is a graduate quality sought by employers. This approach brings team and learning communities back into focus, and will contribute to developing graduates with impact.

Main learning points

❏ Initial time taken to develop the assessment scenario is important. It has considerable payback for the tutors but also, and more importantly, for the student.

❏ Giving students a lot of space to take, and justify, their own direction is time-consuming but ultimately worthwhile in terms of developing graduates with impact.

❏ Removing lectures and much of the scaffolded support students are used to is difficult for some individual students but a good thing if graduates are to 'hit the ground running' in the workplace.

❏ Thinking time, problem solving and practical research skills are important for managers in the workplace – an assessment that develops these in an industry-related scenario will contribute to a graduate's future impact.

❏ The multinational make-up of the student cohorts and the cross-cultural awareness brought out during the module, help further develop the student for a future career in a multi-national business. It also expands the students' repertoire of work-based solutions.

Conclusion

Assessments that enhance graduate impact are not developed in isolation of industrial needs and student engagement. The student engagement comes with an understanding that the assessment is not 'just' an isolated academic exercise but is relevant to their own futures, and provides added value to their future employers in terms of relevant knowledge and ability to provide a service with a shortened learning curve. The notion of relevance to the student is key to engaging them in the learning process.

References and URLs

Aaker, D. (1996) *Building Strong Brands*. The Free Press: New York

Pickford, R. and Brown, S. (2006) *Assessing Skills and Practice*. Abingdon: Routledge

Race, P. and Pickford, R. (2007) *Making Teaching Work: teaching smarter in post-compulsory education*. London: Sage

REAP (2007) *Re-engineering Assessment Practices in Higher Education*. Glasgow, University of Strathclyde. Accessed 7 February 2011 from http://www.reap.ac.uk/

STEVE JONES is principal lecturer in the tourism subject group and teacher fellow at Leeds Metropolitan University. He is currently seconded part-time to the university technology enhanced learning team. Steve's interests include the role of assessments in teaching and learning, computer assisted assessments within the first year learning experience, and audio feedback for formative and summative assessments.

GREIG HEADLEY is undergraduate programme leader in the tourism subject group of Leeds Metropolitan University. He specialises in teaching the marketing strands on the HND and BA International Tourism Management awards. He joined Leeds Metropolitan University in 2000 having previously been tourism marketing officer for South Pembrokeshire, industrial development officer and tourism manager for the Development Board for Rural Wales and manager of the Plymouth Marketing Bureau. He is particularly interested in the development of teaching and learning scenarios that motivate students and prepare them for the world of work.

9

Any volunteers? – an employability case study

Andrea Cameron
University of Abertay, Dundee

A volunteering partnership activity between the University of
Abertay, Dundee (UAD) and Active Schools Dundee has become
an integral part of the first-year sport curriculum. Placement
experiences have been successfully embedded in the UAD
undergraduate sport programmes with an excellent impact on the
local community's engagement with physical activity opportunities.

Introduction

In 2007, a suite of new sport programmes was developed in the Division of Sport
and Exercise Sciences (SES). Applying the principles outlined in the QAA Scotland's
Employability Enhancement theme (QAA, 2007) we decided to make a placement a
compulsory part of each year of study. So the first-year 30-hour placement experience is embedded in a 30-credit double semester module entitled *Contexts in Sport*.
This module allows the students to consider practical applications of theory and to
examine how strands of theory in other parts of the curriculum can be integrated. Six
of the sport programmes start with a common core for the first two years. The experiences in these first and second year modules help students make an informed choice
of specialist pathway to follow at the end of year two, in order to graduate with a
BSc ordinary or honours degree in Strength and Conditioning, Physical Activity and
Health, Sports Coaching, Sports Development, Sport and Exercise Sciences or Sport
and Exercise.

The first-year placement experiences are all organised in association with Active
Schools Dundee (ASD). ASD recruit volunteers to deliver a range of sport and exercise sessions in Dundee schools, with the mission of getting 'more children, more
active, more often'. ASD is funded by both sportscotland (sic) and Dundee City
Council. UAD students are 'volunteered' to form part of the ASD volunteer network;
this provides the students with real experience of sports coaching and leadership,
and ASD with appropriate volunteers.

Placement starts in week six of the student's first semester, and in the weeks before
this, classroom activities prepare the students for placement. Paperwork to allow for a
criminal-record check is completed in induction week to ensure that there is adequate

time to process it before placement begins. Lectures and practical workshops are concentrated on planning, safely delivering, and evaluating activity sessions. Tutorial sessions encourage the students, as part of their Personal Development Plans (PDPs), to set objectives in relation to their placement.

Description

The first-year, first-semester placement is designed to give the students a sports coaching experience and the students are trained by ASD to deliver a six-week *Run, Jump, Throw Club* as an after-school activity targeting ten and eleven-year-old pupils. The six-week block culminates in the identification of pupils to represent their school at a pre-Christmas inter-school athletics festival. The students' training is delivered with the local athletics development officer, and results in the students receiving a Level 1 coaching certificate. Groups of two to three students are allocated a school in which to deliver the programme, under the supervision of an ASD co-ordinator.

The students' timetable is structured so that in the second half of the first semester a dedicated placement slot from three to five p.m. allows them to travel to the school and deliver the session. Practical sessions are still an integral part of the module while students are on placement and during these practical slots students are assessed, as groups, on their ability to teach their peers a sport or exercise activity. Students are provided with instant feedback from module tutors regarding the strengths of the session and also areas requiring development. This information can then be used to enhance the way the student is operating on placement.

The module requires students to attend weekly tutorials at which placement activities are the focus of discussion. Students are encouraged to share their experiences, to discuss any challenges, to reflect on the learning taking place and to consider links between theory and practice. They are also asked to record these reflections in their PDPs, and to consider their progress toward set objectives.

An evaluation of the first *Run, Jump, Throw* programme offered in 2007 demonstrated that over 700 children from 36 primary schools in Dundee took part in the clubs. ASD were able to use this success as an opportunity to promote the existing community *Run, Jump, Throw Clubs*. Attendance at these clubs rose by 200% after the first placement.

Active school placements continue in the second semester, with an emphasis on the links between physical activity and health. The students are trained by ASD to deliver a *Fit Club* package which encourages pupils to consider the links between healthy eating and an active lifestyle. The package is delivered alongside a teacher, to target groups of pupils aged five to nine. Again, the students are given dedicated timetable slots to attend placement, and module practical and tutorial sessions continue to support the students and help them reflect on their learning. Tutorial activities at the end of the module require students to update their curriculum vitae, recording the skills and experience they have gained from placement, as well as articulating this in a personal statement.

The students are also expected to collate their placement experiences in a case study submitted for assessment on completion of the module. Students are not assessed on their delivery of placement sessions but are provided with feedback from ASD co-ordinators and teachers on placement. However, the ASD co-ordinators provide the module tutor with a weekly update of student attendance and of any other issues arising from placement so that supportive remedial action can be taken if necessary.

Figure 9.1 UAD students leading an ASD session

Discussion

Student evaluations of placement are very positive, and placements are regularly identified as the most positive feature of the first year of study. The enthusiasm that the students have for placement has also been recognised by recipients in the school; 'coaches were very enthusiastic' is a frequently cited comment in feedback forms. Isolated negative student comments usually arise from a communication or pupil-behaviour problem, however, even in these cases students are still able to identify that they are learning. Students appreciate the opportunity to be 'out in practice' and also to work with younger client groups, some of whom can have physical and learning difficulties.

In tutorials students frequently voice their surprise at the varying levels of physical literacy, as well as cognitive and physical maturity, evident in similarly aged children. The students also report raised awareness of the social challenges some children face, Dundee being one of the cities targeted by the Scottish Executive in relation to tackling deprivation (Scottish Executive, 2006). The first-year placement is also appreciated for the way in which it can inform second-year placement as well as module choices. It also allows SES to work with a local-authority funded body and increase the volume of physical activity opportunities available to youths in the urban environs of Dundee.

ASD have been able to offer students part- or fully-funded courses leading to coaching qualifications, including those in less mainstream sports, for example, mountain-biking, street dance, skateboarding, and free running. This enables ASD to offer the schools a more varied activity programme, as well as up-skilling the volunteers who are working for them. The students also benefit from these opportunities, as they are then able to add industry-relevant qualifications to their curriculum vitae. In a survey by the programme tutor it was evident that about a quarter of UAD first-year students seek summer employment in vacation activity programmes either at home or abroad, and are able to exploit these experiences to secure seasonal employment.

Evolution

Placement preparation activities have evolved since the outset of the programme as a consequence of feedback from the students, the schools, the module team and the Active Schools co-ordinators. Student enrolment for the UAD sport courses has doubled and this has changed the nature of the ASD placements. Initially the sport programmes had a first-year intake of approximately 100 students. In September 2010 this increased to 219 students, which could have presented a fresh challenge in finding placements. However, an increase in the number of ASD co-ordinators, and in schools requesting ASD programmes, coupled with new partnership activities with the Paediatric Obesity Service for NHS Tayside (POST) and Tennis Tayside, enabled the placements and the module to continue.

Challenges that have arisen with previous student cohorts relate to the reliability of students on placement and the variation in their skill levels, both of which affect the delivery of sessions. The larger intake of students in 2010 meant that a minimum group of three students could be allocated to each activity session. The students were also allocated a partner in week one of the semester and were required to deliver a fifteen-minute sport-skill session to their peers. This allowed the ASD co-ordinators and the module team to differentiate skill level and confidence among the students, and thus to ensure that each of the assigned placement groups included an appropriately skilled member of the first-year cohort. Feedback from students, schools and the ASD co-ordinators suggest that this change has been beneficial and has improved the quality of the placement activity sessions. Comments received from teachers include 'best students so far' and 'I wouldn't know that they were only first-year students'.

In the summer of 2010, ASD and UAD were approached by POST to consider how the current *Fit Club* initiative could be developed to enable POST to work with schools to address weight management issues in primary schoolchildren. The *Fit Club* package was redesigned incorporating new materials and focusing on key health messages that POST wanted the children to grasp. UAD students have been trained to deliver the new programme alongside schoolteachers; there will be an evaluation of this in the summer of 2011. This initiative allows the students to see very clearly how the NHS is working in partnership with local communities to address

Plate 1   The Royal Enclosure at Gondar [Chapter 2]. (*Paul Jackson*)

Plate 2   Gondar [Chapter 2]. (*Elizabeth Draper*)

Plate 3   An Indian market [Chapter 3]. (*Julia Pointon*)

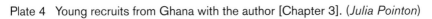

Plate 4   Young recruits from Ghana with the author [Chapter 3]. (*Julia Pointon*)

Plate 5   To celebrate the achievements of the WoW® students, a graduation ceremony was held for both the graduates and current students who had been successful in achieving their WoW® certification [Chapter 4]. (*Liverpool John Moores University*)

Plate 6   The inaugural MUMN Conference, 'Unleashing your potential through mentoring' July 2010. [Chapter 6]. (*Middlesex University*)
Speakers (from left to right) Helen Villalobos *(Lecturer and MA HRD student)*, Nwamaka Onyiuke *(L&D Specialist and MA HRD student)*, Raymond Asumadu *(BA HRM student)*, Julie Haddock-Millar *(Lecturer, HRD)*, Clive Wilson *(Deputy Chairman of Primeast, Ambassador for the Chartered Management Institute)*, Annette Fillery-Travis *(Director, Professional Studies Programmes, IWBL)*, Tulsi Derodra *(BA HRM student)* and Gifty Gabor *(BA HRM student)*.

Plate 7   Three fashion management students discuss the images to present as part of their industry project with John Lewis [Chapter 11]. (*London College of Fashion*)

Plate 8   A Cardiff School of Sport volunteer inspiring the next generation [Chapter 16]. (*CSS*)

health needs.

Tennis Tayside also approached ASD offering to provide funded training for ASD volunteers so that tennis programmes can be offered as part of the ASD activity programme, thus promoting the sport to local children. Thirty first-year and ten second-year students were identified to receive training in January 2011, so that tennis programmes could be offered in the schools' spring term. Again this provides the students with industry-specific qualifications to enhance their curriculum vitae for long-term use, as well as to pick up part-time paid employment.

Moving on

In the second year (Level 5) of the sport programmes the *Contexts in Sport* module continues using the same model of delivery as the first year module and with the students again required to participate in a 30-hour placement. The placement activities are recorded and reflected on in a logbook assessment which is submitted on completion of the module, but PDP work remains an integral part of this module and its experiences.

Students following the BSc (Hons) Sport and Psychology and BSc (Hons) Sport and Exercise Nutrition programmes are invited to undertake a placement with the volunteer agency Dundee Healthy Living Initiative (DHLI). This project is under the auspices of the NHS Scotland *Keep Well* project, which targets 45 to 64-year-old clients at risk of chronic health problems. Physical activity, healthy eating and lifestyle change sessions are delivered to targeted community groups. Students comment on their raised awareness of issues surrounding adherence to health behaviour change and client motivation as a consequence of these experiences. Students have also had the opportunity to undertake *Jog Scotland* Jog Leader and *Paths for All* Walk Leader training programmes to enable DHLI to offer an expanded programme of physical activity sessions.

The other second-year sport students continue placements with ASD, but the placement has a Sports Development theme embedded in it. The students are expected to negotiate the specifics of their 30-hour placement with an ASD co-ordinator – this could involve setting up a new activity club, working with the secondary school sector, or working with first year UAD students on placement.

Evaluation

Through their partnership with UAD, ASD have been able to offer a wide and varied programme across the school sector in Dundee, enabling them to achieve their goals. In 2007–8 as a consequence of the partnership activities Active Schools were able to operate 173,267 participant sessions (one person attending one session, equates to one participant session) in 2009–10 this figure rose to 175,130 participant sessions. However, as detailed in Figure 9.2, this has enabled ASD to be able to offer more early-years sessions, beneficial to both schools and students, allowing younger pupils the opportunity to engage in an active lifestyle and affording students the opportunity to work with children with lower skill levels.

Figure 9.2   Number of participant sessions by age group of children

Total number of participant sessions

Primary School year	08/09	09/10	Percentage +/−
P1	8,096	14,158	+ 42%
P2	10,392	13,675	+ 24%
P3	10,790	14,936	+ 28%
P4	20,481	18,573	− 9%
P5	26,881	29,892	+ 10%
P6	47,653	44,224	− 7%
P7	46,587	39,672	− 17%

The first students from the new suite of the sport programmes have yet to graduate, though some have already progressed to postgraduate teacher-training programmes (the destination for about 15% of UAD sport students). The previous sport programmes also had placement as an integral part of the third year of the programme. Division staff have received favourable feedback from employers and a postgraduate physical education teacher training programme leader about the skills, competency and 'ability to do' of the UAD graduates. The current manager for ASD comments that UAD students have 'a lot of practical and administrative skills as well as a good base of knowledge regarding sport and physical activity'. Currently half of the ASD co-ordinators are UAD graduates, and similar patterns of employment are replicated in other local-authority active-school co-ordinator and sport-development-officer posts.

Commitment, communication and co-ordination have been key to the implementation of this initiative, with the ASD team meeting regularly with the module team to ensure that there is a continued two-way flow of information and that adequate timetable space is given to training. Evaluation is crucial to this process, and since its inception the number of training sessions for placement have increased. Sessions now cover disability-awareness training, as well as managing challenging behaviour, to accompany the more activity specific training sessions.

Enhancing the training remains a feature of placement preparation. While the delivery of the different facets of the initiative can be labour-intensive, the short-term dividends relate to the level of student satisfaction, and the ability to acquire career-specific qualifications and experiences which are used in part-time and seasonal employment. It is hoped that the longer-term dividends will be a continuation of the regard with which UAD sport students are held with local sports employers, as well as employment for the programme's graduates.

A local Disability Sports Development Officer who has had some third and fourth-year UAD students placed with her in recent years comments that she has found the students to be 'absolutely invaluable'. She states that the students have been 'dedicated and committed' and have allowed her 'to enhance service provision'. She further comments that she has found them 'enthusiastic, confident and competent' and 'willing to undertake further training' and the ideas that they have had for how to run sessions and develop the service have been very beneficial.

Conclusion

Aside from increasing the employability prospects of UAD sport graduates this initiative also delivers on the UAD mission of working with and providing for the local community, as well as allowing the programme team to work in partnership with employers ensuring that this group of stakeholders can continue to contribute to curriculum development. Of all the students working in Scotland as volunteers for the Active School network 34% of these are located in Dundee enabling ASD to build a greater capacity for sport in the city.

The module experiences are designed to produce students who are confident and articulate presenters, students who can work as part of a team; and who are aware of, and are able to respond to, challenges in the workplace, as well as having knowledge of issues relevant to the sport and exercise industry. These experiences are built on in the subsequent placement modules, enhancing the students' skillset for the workplace and fostering the UAD graduate attributes of confident thinker, determined creator, flexible collaborator and ambitious enquirer – consequently developing graduates with impact who become assets in the workplace.

References
QAA (2007) *Enhancing Practice – Employability.* QAA, Mansfield
Scottish Executive (2006) *Scottish Index of Multiple Deprivation 2006: General Report.* Scottish
    Executive, Edinburgh
Web-sites/URLs
Active Dundee Dundee's Physical Activity Strategy www.thpc.scot.nhs.uk/PDFs/BVRs/
    Dundee%20Audit.pdf
Active Schools Dundee https://www.dundeecity.gov.uk/chserv/ResourceDets.php?serv_id=831
Dundee Healthy Living Initiative http://www.dundeehealth.com/
Jog Scotland http://www.jogscotland.org.uk/
Paths for All http://www.pathsforall.org.uk/
Paediatric Obesity Service Tayside www.knowledge.scot.nhs.
    uk/.../Putting%20the%20evidence%20into%20practice%20and%20making%20it...
Tennis Tayside http://www.tennistayside.org/

ANDREA CAMERON is the director of academic programmes for the School of Social and Health Sciences at the University of Abertay. Before this, she was programme leader for the BSc (Hons) Sport and Exercise course and she continues to teach the undergraduate sport students, being module tutor for the first and second year **Contexts in Sport** modules and co-ordinating the first and second year sport student placements. She has previously presented and published work in relation to personal development planning and employability initiatives, including **Client in the Classroom.** Before becoming a sport scientist, Andrea was, and remains, a registered nurse (nurse teacher and clinical nurse teacher). She continues to produce patient publications for a diabetes charity. Andrea's interests in heightening skills, competency and employability in graduates derive from her clinical nurse teaching experiences.

ACKNOWLEDGEMENTS
The author would like to acknowledge the contributions of ASD, Dundee City Council and Perth and Kinross City Council in providing images, evaluation data, and employer comments.

10

Developing students into creative managers

Kym Drady *University of Sunderland*
and
Joan Harvey *Newcastle University*

Welcome to a creativity module studied by management undergraduates in their final year. Over 70% of participants claimed a major change in 'the way they think' directly following the experience, several finding their new approach with traditional work-related problems highly productive. This is has also been described by employers locally as highly beneficial. More significantly, a small number of students reported a 'eureka moment' resulting in a complete paradigm shift in their thinking and subsequent work.

Introduction

Today, skills and competences are no longer enough; employers are looking for 'multi-competent graduates' to have impact in their organisations. According to Yorke (2006), they need to be 'future creatives' dealing effectively in social relationships, novel and difficult challenges and they require imagination. They need creative ability to synthesise the bigger picture. Economists see creative individuals as an 'engine for economic growth' and a company's most important asset (Florida and Goodnight, 2006).

Rationale

Weisberg (1993) describes creativity as 'an essentially ordinary cognitive process yielding extra-ordinary products'. Creativity has been investigated for many decades as a notion separate from intelligence: Hudson (1966) investigated how high creativity, when combined with low intelligence, could seriously impact on the subsequent careers of school children when teachers were more comfortable with those who were good at convergent rather than divergent subjects. Sternberg has proposed three categories of intelligence:

❏ *analytical* such as one might find in academic problem-solving
❏ *creative* relating to dealing with new situations
❏ *practical* relating to using existing knowledge and skills (2003: 255).

This case focuses on the last two aspects of this definition, by using existing knowledge in new ways as well as finding entirely new ways to approach tasks and situations. In an educational context, while it may be difficult to define creativity in the context of people aspiring to management positions, it might be said that 'imagining change requires creative thought; and leading change requires creative behaviour' (Harding, 2010).

Hudson (1966) was concerned that schools were rewarding only high intelligence and not high creativity, as the latter made teachers feel uncomfortable and out of control of the children. This raises huge questions about the responsibility of colleges and universities taking on the challenge of introducing creativity into their curriculum. For the theory of pedagogy the concept raises a fundamental point about motivating creativity. Livingstone (2010) believes that 'Humans are inherently creative' and suggests we should not try to teach it, but rather understand, harvest and generate a motivation to embrace it. While we are not asserting here that all people are inherently highly creative, we do believe creativity can be built on and developed, but motivation and self-efficacy beliefs must also be encouraged.

The use of groups has been said to improve performance in many ways, and this can be extended to the concept of self-efficacy and goal orientation such that we can alter our future positively by exercising self-efficacy in order to achieve goals (Bandura and Schunk, 1981). In addition, a safe peer-group environment in an exercise can facilitate 'collective efficacy' that may achieve a greater collective good resulting in positive social evolution and change. (Feldman, Csikszentmihalyi and Garden, 1994).

Case study development

The case study presented here is based on almost ten years' experience of developing and delivering a *Creativity and Innovation* module to final-year undergraduate management students. The cohorts (approximately 15) were mainly part time work-based learners (mature managers and those with supervisory experience), or those looking to pursue a career in management.

The 20-credit module was developed to provide a mix of pedagogical methods comprising traditional lectures, workshops, and one-to-one sessions. The module was delivered for three continuous hours per week for 12 weeks with a residential period of two days at the end. All the sessions contain knowledge and theory elements, integrated with the use of practical hands-on exercises, so that students are working in groups and engaged practically from the outset. The content consists of the following sessions, with about 70% of the emphasis on the first three areas.

❏   What is creativity?
❏   Thinking and problem solving
❏   Creative problem-solving and its various techniques
❏   How to design and facilitate a learning event
❏   Training evaluation
❏   An introduction to the 'personal reflective process'.

The overall aim of the module is to allow students to experience and acquire confidence in engaging in novel and creative activities in order to prepare for the assessment, which takes place during the residential. The brief for the assessment is:

❏ Each student must design and facilitate a 'unique interactive learning event' for his or her peers.

❏ The event is to last no more than 90 minutes (including peer completion of evaluation sheets).

❏ It has to be as original and creative as possible.

❏ The event has to include an evaluation sheet designed for it.

❏ The topic is linked to business management, applied psychology or personal development.

❏ It has to involve interaction for the other student participants.

❏ A plan for the event with clearly stated aims has to be developed and approved at least three weeks before the assessment residential, following individual private consultation with the tutor.

The private consultations have usually been completed between Weeks 6 and 9, after which the tutor used the information to prepare a 'running order' for the assessment events that was as mixed and interesting as possible. With a cohort of 15, this meant that 22½ hours of contact time was needed, in addition to preparation, getting to and from the venue used for the event(s), and the usual refreshment breaks, so the whole residential could run to over two days, although the actual length would be a function of the cohort size.

It is important to present as mixed an agenda as possible, interspersing for example more physical events with mentally stimulating or social-skills ones, and also mixing subject matter and activities. In the residential programme 'running order' each event was given an obscure but relevant title to ensure an element of surprise and anticipation when the actual content was introduced on the day.

Assessment of this type of student activity presents issues in itself, as there is no real template when such diverse events are developed, and how to put a value on novelty and creativity? The assessment comprises two elements:

Section A, assessed during the residential session, is worth 50% and the tutor rates the student on:

❏ originality of the event

❏ use of literature and resources in relation to creativity

❏ use of literature and resources in the chosen topic area

❏ planning and facilitation of the event

❏ the design of the evaluation form.

Section B is assessed after the residential and is worth 50% of the overall mark: students are rated on:

❏ their reflective report of the event

❏ the extent to which the event met its stated aims

❏ an action plan for future modifications.

In order to facilitate the report, enable recall and subsequent re-use of any events in the workplace, still photos were taken throughout all the residential events and students were presented with a CD of both their personal event and summary photos of all other sessions and events, containing on average 15 to 20 photos. They were encouraged to use this photographic diary when reflecting on their event. Feedback received on these assignments from the external examiners has been outstanding and the module has been singled out for its innovation and originality in teaching, learning and assessment.

Several key considerations need to be addressed to ensure the best results, the first being the actual physical environment. Here, the crucial open creative environment was facilitated for each cohort by the use of a residential hotel space which allowed students an empty room space to customise with their own materials and props relevant to the environment for their event. This approach promotes risk-taking and confidence, two essential elements in creativity, following Kleinman (2008) and Kao's (1996) notions that attention to the physical working space 'physically and interactionally' improves creativity.

The second element to consider is the group and the creation of a safe environment, one which encourages self-efficacy, experimentation and challenges conventionality, in which the students gain confidence in working with one another, but also is conducive to dealing with uncertainty and complex problem-solving. Several exercises were used for this purpose during the 12 three-hour sessions, all of which introduce novelty, challenge and diversity of thinking and pave the way for 'framing' (Kao, 1996).

The third element is the students' understanding of the creative process and 'framing' in order to develop their own personal events in the residential. Although the residential idea is introduced during week one, students can only start to frame their ideas for their own sessions once they have an understanding of problem-solving and how creative play can enhance this. The individual sessions with each student need to be conducted away from the class, at a point when the students have had ideas ready to discuss for their own session and in time for each idea to be declared and approved.

An aspect of this programme has been its unpredictability in terms of what ideas the students generate, since there can be no prescription for the students' events other than that they must meet the requirements of the brief. As a consequence, the events will vary from novel ways to address well-known problems to those that are highly original: so far, these have been variously aimed at teambuilding, communications, disability awareness, collaboration and competition. Some examples have included:

❏ The design of a metaphor representing the tutor's characteristics, demonstrated by using the Johari Window from creative materials provided.

❏ Addressing the HR issue of managing people with schizophrenia, by using long cardboard tubing to communicate odd messages while role-playing an everyday interview.

- ❏ A new method of teaching motivation, contrasting the experience of making peppermint creams in a cottage industry with that of a Taylorist factory environment managed by time and motion.
- ❏ A *University Challenge* style quiz with a rigged buzzer to introduce an ethics event, in a very competitive group.
- ❏ The development of a new board game for health and fire safety training.
- ❏ Soft play equipment to illustrate the management concepts of collaboration and competition.

Evaluation of findings

Over the ten-year period, changes and adjustments were made to improve the module as a result of feedback information from both students and tutor. The relaxed hotel environment for the residential assessment improved interaction and confidence building compared to whole in-college days. Later developments included the addition of tools to help students to facilitate their own event, including input on training design and evaluation. Considering the whole process (including the now embedded changes, the feedback, external examiners reports and comments from employers) suggests that the overall aims of the module – to get students to experience and engage in creative problem solving – are met fully.

Feedback has been collected throughout the module, in both formal and informal ways. Formal feedback was obtained using module sheets as part of the course review process, but there have also been the reflective reports as part of the assessments. Informal feedback came from student comments and, after the course, employers' comments. All are highly positive with two main themes emerging,

Confidence

For many students, the facilitation of their own event was a completely new experience and clearly improved their levels of self-confidence. For all of them, including those already more experienced as facilitators, the opportunity to see up to 14 other events delivered in a host of different ways clearly broadened their experience and encouraged their ideas for adoption of new methods. The students' lead in teaching and understanding creativity and the creativity experience itself increased personal confidence in their own ability. This reportedly transferred to, and was demonstrated, at work.

Ability to think

Without exception students reported that the module made them 'look at objects and situations in a new light', seeing new opportunities they would not have identified before. In a specific but not unique example this enhanced thinking led to a manager from the NHS completely re-organising the way she managed her department, resulting in massive cost savings and increased effectiveness against key performance targets that she had previously struggled to meet. She believes she had a 'eureka' experience following the module. Her line manager reported her as 'a changed if not slightly mad excited woman' who made major changes to his organisation, with which philosophy she still persists some nine year later. Several such cases have been cited in subsequent interviews of longer term effects across different sectors such as in local authorities, the IT industry and in commerce.

Discussion

The evidence from this programme suggests very clearly that teaching creativity to management students can have major benefits, from generating more insightful graduates right through to those who experience a major paradigm shift in the way they think and act.

So far, only immediate feedback and follow-up has been conducted, so it is not possible to say how long lasting the effects will be, apart from the nine-year example above. It may be the students' workplace environments can build on these changes and really move forward, or returning to the status quo may make this more difficult or even impossible. We suggest that some sort of follow-up activity would be of value, such as bringing the cohorts back to an annual 'event' of some sort. The immediate next stage for this course is to contact past students and either by interview or questionnaire ascertain how useful the programme has turned out to be subsequently.

The events themselves did not always 'go to plan'; however, each did provide a wealth of issues to discuss, including how such psychological issues such as group-think, team working, communication failures, and non-verbal communications on the part of the participants contributed to the success or otherwise of the event, and the importance of planning realistic aims and interactive processes while retaining a focus on outcomes.

An example of how something not going to plan can generate a really informative discussion was when soft-play equipment was used in a session in which group-think led participants to ignore simple instructions that required them to collaborate before they could compete to complete the task. Only after this collaborative element of the process was eventually recognised did the planned competitive element commence. This example is one of a novel approach to look at a traditional problem [collaborate first, compete later] but where subsequent discussion allowed the group to consider how the process could be modified for the future.

There does not appear to be one single success factor in this approach to teaching creativity. Instead, we propose a gestalt-type approach, in that it is the sum that is bigger than the parts here. It is the combination of learning and practice through the whole experience, and the individual and team efficacy, that facilitate the development of creative problem-solving, all set in a confidence-building situation free from any threat to self-esteem.

Learning points
- ❏ This course seems to develop creative problem-solving very effectively.
- ❏ All students on all ten cohorts have cited benefits of at least insight and right up to 'eureka' moments.
- ❏ Employers like the way students who complete this programme are more able to take on new approaches to problems.
- ❏ This course is moderately labour-intensive to run. It involves, for fifteen students, direct class contact of around 75 hours plus time for the preparation of teaching materials, the CD and the assessments.
- ❏ The course can only really work with smaller cohorts.
- ❏ The course requires a tutor who can handle the uncertainty of not knowing what will be in the residential, or how it will work, until the time itself.
- ❏ The course is best suited to students with some prior work experience, or part-time management students who are also working.
- ❏ It may be possible to get some local employers to provide some support, e.g. in terms of facilities.
- ❏ A residential approach to the assessment increases self-confidence to experiment.

Conclusion

While we cannot say for sure how long the effects last, the module clearly does have an impact on the students on completion of the course and for several years thereafter. It would appear that this impact is predominantly on decision-making, and therefore it may be that the students who benefit most have a position in their work that allows this level of authority. Two major reasons for the success of this programme seem to be the facility to try completely new ideas out without fear or risk, and to be exposed to a wide variety of other, often very different, ideas emanating from the same process.

References

Bandura, A. and Schunk, D. (1981) Cultivating Competence: Self-Efficacy and Intrinsic Interest through Proximal Self-Motivation. *Journal of Personality and Social Psychology* 41 (3) 686–98

Feldman, D., Csikszentmihalyi, M. and Gardner, H. (1994) *Changing the World: A Framework for the study of Creativity*. New York: Praeger

Florida, R. and Goodnight, J. (2006) Managing for Creativity *Harvard Business Review* 83 (7) 124–32

Harding, T. (2010), Fostering Creativity for Leadership and Leading Change. *Arts Education Policy Review* 111 51–3

Hudson, L. (1966) *Contrary Imaginations: A Psychological Study of the English Schoolboy*. London: Methuen

Kao, J. (1996) *Jamming: The Art and Discipline of Business Creativity*. Harper Collins

Kleiman, P. (2008) Towards transformation: conceptions of creativity in higher education. *Innovations in Education and Teaching International* 45 (3) 209–17

Livingston, L. (2010) Teaching Creativity in Higher Education. *Arts Education Policy Review* **111** 59-62

Sternberg, R. J. (2003) *Handbook of Creativity*. Cambridge: Cambridge University Press 255

Weisberg, R. W. (1993) *Creativity: Beyond the myth of genius*. New York: Freeman

Yorke, M. (2006) Employability in Higher Education: What it is and what it's not. In M Yorke (ed), *Learning and Employability*, Series 1. York: Learning Teaching and Support Network

KYM DRADY is a senior lecturer in HRM at the University of Sunderland. She has experience of delivering HE both in a college of further education and the University. She has extensive experience of management training both in education and also in the commercial sector. She is currently seeking to broaden her research as she has recently enrolled on a PhD programme within the University.

JOAN HARVEY is a Chartered Psychologist at Newcastle University. She has experience in management training and development and in short-term training, undergraduate and postgraduate management education. She has written on the evaluation of management training and motivation and values of management, and is currently supervising a DBA student in developing new means of making management training more likely to result in long-term behaviour change.

Grateful thanks are offered to Dr Gail Sanders from the University of Sunderland for help in editing the proposal.

11

Shaping future fashion leaders

Liz Gee and Heather Pickard
London College of Fashion

The chapter that follows illustrates how curriculum content can be carefully constructed to maximise industry relationships and ensure that graduates make real impact throughout their careers.

Introduction

At the London College of Fashion, a constituent college of the University of the Arts London, our prestigious course, BA (Honours) Fashion Management (BAFM) has over 400 students, approximately 120 students in each of the three Year groups, and over 40 students out on placement in industry. With a ratio of over 11 applications for each place, the course goes from strength to strength.

The recession has served to sharpen the focus of many institutions on employability. This course views employability as not just about equipping our students with transferable skills but is also about empowering our students to have a positive 'can do' attitude.

Industry links

The tutor team work closely with industry at many levels. An industry forum is held regularly to ensure the currency of course content and that our graduates' skills continue to remain relevant to the workplace.

From the student's perspective, the industry partnership starts in the first year and builds to become central to the placement year; an optional sandwich year in industry or study abroad at the end of the second year which leads to a stand-alone qualification, the *Diploma in Professional Studies*.

Every week professionals active in the industry speak to the students on a particular live challenge facing their business; be it refreshing a tired brand or seizing the opportunities offered by mobile commerce (m-commerce). By attending this programme, our first year (Level 4) students are gaining invaluable first hand business awareness from industry professionals in a context that is highly relevant to their studies and future career prospects

Embedding knowledge and skills

The key to ensuring that our graduates have impact once out in the workplace centres around the multiple opportunities provided to put their knowledge into practice across each of the stages of their degree. In terms of embedding skills and knowledge the key is 'application, application, application'.

In the third term of the first year the students work in small teams on a fashion management project. Currently the theme of this project centres on leveraging the opportunity of the London Olympics for a sports fashion brand. This project gives the students the first opportunity to put into practice the theory they have learned in the first two terms. This is related to buying and merchandising, marketing and retailing product and the associated financial and people resource issues.

What our students say   1

All staff have a lot of industry experience and maintain excellent contacts with industry. A lot of what we do is related to real life; in general I am pleased with the course.

Content of course & extra opportunities the university provides (e.g. internships, visiting speakers).

The content of the course was excellent. There are a few star lecturers. As a result of the course, I feel I have a wealth of knowledge. I think I would choose it all over again despite its flaws.

Live work-based projects

At the end of their second year (Level 5) of study, students work in pairs, taking on the role of business consultants in a unit entitled *Fashion Consultancy Project* (FCP). They approach fashion businesses of their choice to work in partnership on live business projects. Clients may be large or small, well known or obscure and the issue to be addressed is a real business problem. Every year the students engage with up to 50 different fashion companies pursuing these projects which range from working with small independent boutiques on their visual merchandising and marketing, to working with larger companies designing and monitoring their websites, through to working with major plcs on research into the launch of a new range.

Student profile 1   Rebecca

Rebecca and another student worked with Mio Destino a designer swimwear and underwear brand for their FCP. They helped the brand launch a premium quality mastectomy lingerie range by undertaking research surveying the views and attitudes of over 100 women and breast-cancer care nurses. They then worked with the brand through to the launch of the Di Murini range. Rebecca then went on placement to Hong Kong working with supply-chain consultants and excelled in her third year graduating with a first-class honours degree.

Globalisation affects us too

Interestingly, as figure 11.1 shows, more than half the new intake of students enrolling onto BAFM this year are classed as international students, mainly of Asian origin (see figure 11.2). This is a slight increase on the course three-year average of 50% home and EU and contrasts with the UAL base of 60.3% home, 13.3% EU and 26.4% international.

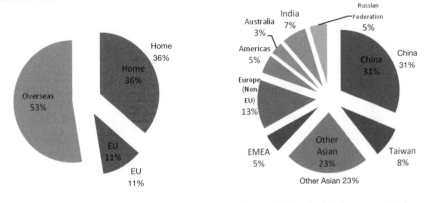

Figure 11.1   2010 Intake by origin   Figure 11.2   2010 Overseas intake

The course team work hard to ensure that the team projects in the first year are comprised of a balance of home/EU and overseas students. It is important that the nationalities mix and share with each other the benefits of their different cultural perspectives.

Such a diverse cohort produces numerous challenges: group dynamics and a spectrum of language skills being the most prominent. Dedicated language support is embedded throughout the curriculum and additional support provided at key points during the year to overcome some of these key communication issues.

In addition, the course continues to develop links with specific international academic institutions to enable exchanges of students. This serves to ensure a cultural diversity throughout the later years of the course and helps foster debate in final year (Level 6) case study strategy classes. A recent example of this can be seen in a Uniglo brand case study. Perspectives were offered by students with first-hand experience of their retail operations in Russia, France and Japan; they were also able to give an appreciation of how entrenched the Japanese culture is in the brand and the vision of its leaders.

A solid foundation

The learning journey at UAL starts with a common unit in the first term in which students learn underpinning skills, such as research, how to make effective presentations and essay and report writing – key transferable skills that are deemed vital for their academic and career success. The content of this unit is developed and expanded in BAFM with a focus on numeracy skills and ICT confidence, to ensure that the skills learned underpin students' future business success.

The teaching team constantly seek to develop the course by introducing new technologies and simulation software such as 'Mock Shop,' which allows students to design a store in 3D from the lighting and signage, to the fixtures and changing rooms. Such technology enhances the learning experience, allowing the students to put theory into practice in a simulation of tasks they will need to tackle in their careers. Many of our course team, the teaching and course management staff, not just visiting tutors, come from industry backgrounds and have themselves experienced the roles to which our students aspire. Our students dream of becoming a head of merchandising at Debenhams or director of buying of one of the Arcadia brands. They emerge from this degree course well-prepared and well-equipped to begin that career journey.

Getting the most from a sandwich

While there has been a UK wide decline in traditional sandwich courses, BAFM has retained this important element leading to a qualification in its own right – the *Diploma in Professional Studies*. Through the dedicated role of an industrial placement tutor working closely with colleagues in our fashion business resource studio, the relationship with industry is formalised to guarantee that every placement benefits both the student and the employer. Placements are sourced across a whole spectrum of fashion companies from Prada, Burberry and Mulberry to Superdry, Marks & Spencer and George at Asda.

A relationship with the business is cemented via formal contracts. A programme of progress visits is undertaken and the students complete progress logs and a placement report.

Student Profile 2   Beth

For her second year consultancy project, Beth and her partner worked with Asda performing research leading to the launch of a new range of children's clothes. Beth then went on placement at Marks and Spencer in 2009 where she worked as Store Manager in a busy outer London shopping centre. Her manager spoke of her as 'a valued and respected member of the senior management team'. She rose to the challenges laid before her and took 'real ownership getting a true feeling of accountability for profit and all aspects of people management'. Her personal drive and positive approach were also commended and she will be considered for future opportunities in the business following her final year.

The placement year is recommended to all students who satisfy the prerequisites of having excellent studentship credentials and the available financial resources, as it not only advances skills and technical expertise but also engenders confidence and maturity. However, it is recognised that for varying reasons, placement cannot be the choice of all students. The reasons are often financial as many of the industry placements are unpaid. Whether they are planning to undertake the placement year or continue directly with their studies, all students participate in an extensive 'preparation for industry' programme in the second year which includes CV-writing, job-search skills and selection-interview practice.

Placement students see many benefits aside from those which directly relate to their future employability from working in industry for a year. They appreciate the contacts that they make and the opportunity to put into practice the theory they have learned, but also they cite the impact the year away from study makes on their final year. They are not only exposed to issues that could form commercially realistic dissertation topics but are also well versed in coping strategies – from working under pressure and to deadlines – which stand them in good stead for the case study exams. It is true that some find it hard to get back into the role of being a student again, but when we map placement students against final degree class we see an interesting pattern emerge (see figure 3) in which 87% of placement students achieve a first or upper-second-class degree compared to 50% of non-placement students.

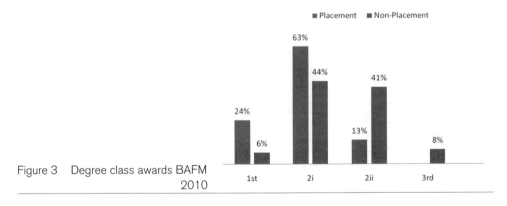

Figure 3   Degree class awards BAFM 2010

Not only but also

Employers undoubtedly want graduates with relevant experience of the workplace. In addition to the placement year, our students are encouraged to take internships throughout their studies to enable them to test what they are learning in the workplace and appreciate the relevance of their studies. These graduates are more able to take a proactive approach to their career management as they have already experienced various real life roles and have developed a highly relevant CV.

What our students say 2
The emphasis on career path planning and the emphasis on the working environment

were very good.

Preparation for industry second to none – e.g. CVs, presentation skills & practical learning. FCP – very enjoyable, preparations, interesting project.

It's very career-focused and you learn a lot of skills for the workplace.

Contacts and resources; active encouragement with the placements.

Demonstrating the difference

Final degree classification is determined largely by an individual dissertation. For several years the course has been fortunate in maintaining a relationship with the major UK fashion retailer Oasis, which sponsors prizes for the best three dissertations. The judges include academic faculty, representatives of the Oasis Board of Directors and a key figure from WGSN, an important player in the fashion trade press. Students focus on commercial research underpinned by academic theories, but the end result is that these higher-level works are incredibly relevant to the future direction of the fashion industry and without a doubt have real impact. It is no coincidence that the winners of these prizes are often ex-placement students, as these students often present a more mature and commercially aware approach to their final year studies.

Student Profile 3   Jessica

Jessica spent her placement year at Debenhams, where she excelled in many areas and was valued as a significant part of the women's wear team. She graduated with a first-class degree after writing an excellent dissertation on the significance of the older female consumer. This was judged at the Association of Suppliers to the British Clothing Industry (ASBCI) awards in November 2010 and Jessica was awarded second place. Immediately following the completion of the course, Jessica returned to Debenhams and is now well on the way to completing her training as a trainee assistant buyer in the very important occasion wear and evening wear departments.

Trial by case study

A fashion-business case study is the other significant element of the final-year assessment. Good marks and often degree class are achieved by the excellent application of models and concepts to the company studied using the case study method. The case-study company is selected and the detailed case written each year by a small team of tutors. They highlight relevant current issues faced by that particular company, and the fashion industry in a more holistic sense. Some of the companies which have been used in recent years include Dior, Next, Burberry, Abercrombie & Fitch, ASOS and this year Uniqlo.

Why BA Fashion Management works

Modern student life, especially in London, encourages 'strategic' learning out of necessity. The financial pressures coupled with the need to obtain relevant work experience can be a double-edged sword. Many students work long hours in highly pressurised retail environments so they are time-poor and often tired and inattentive when it comes to focusing on their academic studies. The use of learning outcomes helps students focus on what they need to achieve so they can target their study. Tutors see this manifest itself as less 'reading around' the subject, and the need for them to give clear direction in assignment guidelines as there is no doubt that assessment lies at the heart of the student experience.

The learning outcomes and assignments are carefully constructively aligned (Biggs, 2006). Every attempt is made to stagger assignment deadlines to avoid assessment overload, which can create surface learning. The constant application of theory to real world scenarios in itself is encouraging a deep approach to learning (Biggs, 2006), with the case study ensuring students understand the theories at a relational level, if only in one organisation. Good performance in a case-study exam means demonstrating the higher skills (Bloom, 1964) of analysis, synthesis, criticism, argument and relational level thinking.

Understanding is personal and not something we can transmit. As tutors we can give students the structure to help them organise the material and make connections (Marton et al, 1984). It is what the learner has to do (i.e. learning activities) to construct knowledge that is important; these activities are framed in the context of the real world with anecdotes and examples. How students seek to understand partly depends on their prior knowledge much of which is gained via employment or experience of work. Ramsden's conceptualisation of the deep approach as 'energetically searching for meaning' is more meaningful than simply 'activity', which could be aimless (2003).

At UAL we believe it is important to complete the experiential learning cycle (Kolb, 1984) in order to develop learning, and to build on knowledge and experience.

Figure 4   A fashion management student presents a mood board as part of an industry project run in partnership with John Lewis
(LCF)

Reflective tasks are embedded in every unit in Year One (Level 4) so that the benefit is clearly appreciated and reflection becomes an automatic part of learning rather than yet another task. Reflection is most valuable in experiential learning situations such as the placement year, the fashion consultancy project (FCP), or where the unit draws on vastly different skills, for example, group work or individual dissertation. The value of reflection on academic content itself lies in the reframing of the subject matter in a personal context to construct meaning and understanding.

We know students look to their tutors to identify their study objectives and criteria for judgement and this in turn encourages dependence. In encouraging independent learners we want them to appreciate how to learn so they can monitor their own work, establish their own criteria and make judgements about their achievements. These 'transformative' skills (Harvey & Knight, 1996) closely link reflection, deep learning and self-assessment, an essential graduate skill where self-awareness is linked to employability, enabling them to continue on their lifelong learning journey without formal course structure and tutor intervention. Only by knowing what you know and knowing what you don't, but should know, can you identify the gaps in your learning and take steps to fill them.

Notions of co-operative learning and reciprocity run through the third year of the course. Peer learning is encouraged to ensure the students returning from placement share their experiences of the working environment and, in return, benefit from the students who have come straight from Year Two where the academic theory may be more accessible in their minds. Boud et al characterise peer learning as a 'two-way reciprocal learning activity' where there is equal power and mutual benefit for both parties involved (2001:3). The peer-learning experience involves the group sharing ideas, experience and knowledge and emphasises interdependent rather than independent learning (Boud et al, 2001). This is facilitated in the early stages of Year Three when dissertation proposals are discussed in group workshops.

The students are all helping each other by sharing ideas and experiences, putting new perspectives forward to help solve problems. Students are encouraging and enabling each other's achievement and understanding, collaborating to construct new meaning. In having to explain their ideas to others, they are crystallising their thoughts into words, improving their communication skills and reconstructing their own understanding.

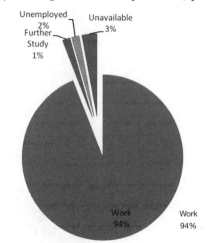

Figure 5 DLHE BAFM 2009

BAFM is not perfect and is hidebound by UAL policy where only the final year counts towards the final degree classification. There is no doubt achievement would be better if a small proportion of Year Two marks could count towards the degree class; this would reduce a tendency for assessment to drive learning in the third year.

Onwards and upwards

Students are entering the toughest graduate jobs market in over a decade, with official statistics showing graduate unemployment on the rise. It is no wonder that they see themselves as customers. A 'good value for money' degree has to be one that leaves them well equipped to find work on graduation. To them the destination of leavers (DLHE) statistics are far more relevant than institutional scores on student satisfaction surveys and any government requirement to make available statistics on graduate destinations and earnings should be welcomed.

Of our class of 2009, figure 4 above shows a healthy employment ratio. Fifteen of our graduates became fashion buyers, 14 entered other training schemes with several major fashion retailers, 11 took retail management positions and six are employed in marketing roles. Of the employers, four went to work with Marks and Spencer, three with Burberry, two with Harrods, two with Debenhams, two with House of Fraser and one each to Harvey Nichols and John Lewis; there are many others not listed here. Of those employed many were earning salaries in excess of £20,000.

The University of the Arts London has the dubious accolade of featuring in last place on the National Student Survey. That horrifying statistic masks the true performance of the BAFM degree course where scores of a 72% overall satisfaction rating were reported in 2010. 91% of our final year students expressed satisfaction with their final year experience.

Student Profile 4   Sarah

Sarah went on placement in Hong Kong in 2007. After writing a first-class dissertation on 'tweenage' clothing she graduated straight into a buyer's role at the Disney store. Rapid promotion to head buyer followed and in November 2010 she has been headhunted again. Her career is certainly on an upward trajectory.

As one of the newest collegiate members of the Association of Business Schools we see our graduates leave us as true business school graduates. Indeed many business school scholars envy our position. Our graduates have spent three or possibly four years applying generic management concepts to the highly dynamic fashion industry; it is no wonder they have impact and get off to a flying start in the fashion business world. BAFM will continue to nurture its dialogue with the major graduate employers in the fashion business. We must work in partnership with business to continue to be relevant to our students who are ever more driven by the jobs they aspire to, rather than a love of learning their subject.

References

Biggs, J. (2006) *Teaching for Quality Learning at University: Second Edition*. Buckingham: SHRE and Open University Press

Bloom (1964) in Reece, I. and Walker, S. (2003) *Teaching, Training and Learning: a practical guide*, 5th edition. Sunderland: Business Education Publishers

Boud, D., Keogh, R. and Walker, D. (2001) *Reflection: Turning Experience into Learning*. London: Kogan Page

Harvey, L. and Knight, P. (1996) *Transforming Higher Education*. Buckingham: SHRE and Open University Press

Kolb, D. (1984) *Experiential Learning*. London: Prentice Hall

Marton, F., Hounsell, D. and Entwistle, N. (eds) (1984) *The Experience of Learning*. Edinburgh: Scottish Academic Press

Ramsden, P. (2003) *Learning to Teach in Higher Education*. London: Routledge

LIZ GEE studied psychology at the University of Bristol and then went on to train as a chartered accountant with one of the 'Big Four' firms, Ernst & Young in London. After qualification she moved straight out to industry, joining internal audit at The Burton Group (now Arcadia). Several years of different finance-manager roles later as Debenhams plc de-merged from the Group, Liz went on to be corporate treasurer. In time, Liz decided it was time for a new challenge at Barclays Bank plc where as a relationship director she was responsible for the corporate banking affairs of many retail and wholesale fashion clients including Liberty, Select, Hawes & Curtis and Blue Inc to name just a few. Soon a few hours as a visiting lecturer at the London College of Fashion became a full time role as Liz brought her practical finance experience from all types of companies to life in the classroom. Liz is a fellow of the Higher Education Academy.

HEATHER PICKARD took a geography degree at the University of Sussex and has been involved with the fashion industry for over 25 years. She joined Top Shop as a retail management trainee before moving over to head office and swiftly moved up the career ladder of The Burton Group (now Arcadia) to the role of senior merchandiser. As a buying and merchandising controller her fashion and management experience grew at Laura Ashley, Sock Shop and River Island before her career changed direction and she joined the London Institute, now the University of the Arts, London. Her teaching inputs on a variety of courses from further education, undergraduate and postgraduate draws on her experience of supply chain and buying and merchandising. This was used in the work she did establishing the curriculum for the Fashion Retail Academy, the first private/ government funded academy devoted to a specific industry sector. Furthermore, her current role as Programme Director, Management, exploits all the management skills acquired in industry. Heather brings a great deal of overall real life experience to all aspects of her work at the London College of Fashion.

12

From small changes to maximum impact
Food and Nutrition Students improve public health

Kevin Nield and Trevor Simper
Sheffield Business School, Sheffield Hallam University

This chapter examines how student project work, a 'Small Changes' programme involving food and nutrition students, can enhance the health of the public. The project also provides students with the skills needed to obtain employment in the broad area of nutrition and wellbeing. Projects like this, properly run and supervised, can provide benefits to the public, the university and employers as well as helping create graduates with impact.

Introduction

Small Changes was originally funded by All Saint's Education Trust which funds projects aimed at improving nutrition education and furthering skills around food and cooking. The idea for the project came from Trevor Simper and Jean O'Keeffe, a public health nutritionist and the director of a charity dealing in weight management (both now employed by the department of service sector management). *Small Changes* developed during a two-year pilot period in Keighley in West Yorkshire.

At Sheffield Hallam the idea was to attach academic rigour to the project, create a research base for it, and involve the final year nutrition and food students in delivering sessions, gathering data, and evaluation. They would also be working for *Small Changes*.

Participants with a body mass index of greater than $30kg/m^2$ (the point at which people are described as obese and at much greater risk for health problems such as diabetes and heart disease) were recruited by a newspaper advertisement and internet forum and invited to Sheffield Hallam to an open event. Staff and students carried out assessments at the event to determine those who met the BMI criteria and had no chronic pre-existing health issues that precluded them from participating.

Rationale

Issues concerning obesity and weight management are currently a major issue in health and well-being (Foresight, 2007). The students involved in the *Small Changes* project are aspiring to careers in the health and wellbeing and/or lifestyle sectors of the economy. It is part of the mission of the Sheffield Business School at Sheffield Hallam to provide students with the necessary skills and experience to be employable in graduate level jobs. The school wishes further to make an impact on its local community by providing the knowledge and services that it requires. The small changes project allows the students and the university to provide major benefits and impact on its local community while providing real life experiences for its students.

Context

Sheffield Hallam University is the largest provider of food and nutrition higher education in the UK. At present there are over 450 undergraduate and postgraduate students studying food and nutrition courses in the Sheffield Business School. The majority of these students are undergraduates, studying on one of three degrees in Food and Nutrition, Public Health Nutrition, or Nutrition, Health and Lifestyles. The student body is predominantly female; the ratio of females to males is approximately 80:20. There is a small but growing number of international students. The courses show success in student satisfaction measurements, and are often used to benchmark good practice across the university. The nutrition courses received the highest satisfaction scores and were ranked number one in their subject area in the 2010 National Student Survey (NSS) with an overall satisfaction score at an astounding 97%!

The vast majority of the students leave to become food and nutrition professionals in both the public and private sectors, working primarily in the health service and in the lifestyle sector. There is a high level of take-up of these students in what is categorised in the league tables as graduate level employment.

One of the most successful of these interventions is the *Small Changes* programme. This chapter will feature the *Small Changes* programme and its part in the final year project module.

Description

The *Small Changes* programme

The programme is aimed at groups of individuals from the general public in Sheffield and South Yorkshire who wish to make positive changes to their personal health and wellbeing. Rather than merely being an advice service that tells people what to eat and how to exercise, the *Small Changes* programme is a support mechanism that works 'in the context' of people's lives. So 'small changes' are part of what people do on a daily basis, not something added on to or outside their normal behaviour.

The simple but effective idea behind the project is that, by making small changes to their lifestyles, and by becoming involved in the *Small Changes* weight management/lifestyle change programme, individuals and groups are able to produce major benefits to their own health and wellbeing. Figure 1 shows the content of the 12-week curriculum employed by *Small Changes*.

As can be seen, the crux of the programme is that people are helped to make their own choices around changing diet and exercise to improve their health. These

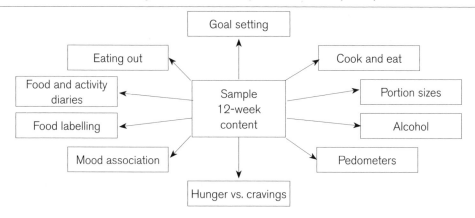

Figure 1 Small Changes project sample content

changes may be as simple as wearing a pedometer and targeting the number of steps that should be taken each day, or keeping a food diary so that the quantity and type of food that is eaten is recorded. None of these interventions constitute a major change; they are merely 'small changes' that may eventually lead to major changes in lifestyle. The important thing is that these changes are sustainable and that they are likely to work for the individual. This is made more probable because each person has chosen the change they will make, rather than being told to do something.

Management of the *Small Changes* programme

The programme is managed by the tutors and students as part of a wider final year project. Under the supervision of a tutor each student takes anthropometric (body fat, cholesterol, blood sugar, height/weight) measurements, delivers education sessions and produces a thesis based on one of these measurements for their final year project. To give the time that is required for such an undertaking the students are organised into learning sets whose numbers are kept low; there are normally five students in each learning set. In 2009–10 there were ten students in two learning sets working on *Small Changes* projects at undergraduate level and three more at postgraduate level.

The advantages of the learning sets are that the students:-
1 Are very closely supervised – as a consequence ethical and health and safety issues may be closely monitored.
2 Meet on a very regular basis both formally and informally; there is ample opportunity for feedback/forward on all aspects of the students' work.
3 Learn from each other as students report back on what they have done.
4 Receive more supervision due to the economies of the learning set.

The success of the projects and the *Small Changes* programme may be measured in two ways: from the feedback of the people who participate in the programme, and from the students' recognition of the benefits that they have received. However, the success of these projects can also be measured by some of the external recognition bestowed on them. Two of the students who worked on the projects are now full-time employees carrying out research and teaching with the university and both have won outstanding achievement awards.

The programme makes students aware of the development of their employability skills by asking them to keep a reflective diary, an assessed piece of work in which they reflect on employability over the course of the year. They are given Knight and Yorke's (2004) list of employability skills, asked to choose one of the sets of skills and comment on how these have improved over the first semester. They are then asked to repeat this for a different set of skills in the second semester. Finally, they are asked to identify their weaknesses and write an action plan of how they intend to overcome these on entering employment. As part of the learning-set process students are asked to bring their diaries to some of the learning-set meetings.

A typical *Small Changes* project

Weight management is a serious problem in South Yorkshire where rates of obesity and related diseases are above the national average and where it is statistically normal to be overweight. Recently, people with high body mass indexes from South Yorkshire were offered a free *Small Changes* course and a grant application was made to fund the project; £89,000 was awarded by the All Saints Educational trust to carry out the *Small Changes* work.

In a *Small Changes* project, the changes to lifestyle are agreed with the client; this intervention is then monitored across the duration of the project, normally 12 weeks. Typically, a maximum of 10 participants take part in weekly two-hour sessions, some of which are run by the students, in a learning set supervised by a member of academic staff. Monitoring of the project gives real-life learning as students, under supervision, measure anthropometrics, (such as weight, waist measurement), blood measures (such as cholesterol) and lifestyle and wellbeing factors.

However, it should be remembered that the plan is the client's and this is what makes the intervention effective. As client A said

> It is not a specific plan which has been made up for everybody, it's your own plan you make up.

Client B reinforces this by saying

> I think that the fact that you are in control and can choose your small changes, you choose what you are going to eat, makes a big difference so therefore you feel more in control of what you are doing.

Evaluation and discussion

This section will examine the work of some of the learning sets of five students who took part in the *Small Changes* programme in 2009–10. The projects are evaluated from the points of view of the students who took part, the clients who participated and employers who oversaw some of the projects. The evaluation considers the impact on the general public, on the students involved, on the university and on employers. It uses mainly qualitative data based on the students' reflections on their learning from the intervention, the clients' on the impact of the intervention on their personal wellbeing, and reflections from employers on the abilities and employability of the students.

Impact on the public

At the end of their 12-week sessions clients who took part in the *Small Changes* programme were asked to comment on the programme, how it had operated and the impact on their health and well being.

Physical wellbeing and self-monitoring

Many of the clients reported that they felt much better physically and had gone some way to achieving better health. In a study that had put in interventions aimed at preventing coronary heart disease, participants reported that they now understood the condition, and importantly, as one of them said:

> a lot of us have watched our cholesterol drop down which I think was a very serious health issue so that has been really good and very remarkable.

Self-monitoring was also seen as crucial to ensure that clients were able to understand and achieve the desired result. A client reflected on using the food diary in which she wrote down everything that she ate, and said

> the power of writing things down and doing a food diary really amazed me – how much impact it made to me seeing what I had eaten from looking at what I had written down on paper.

Goal achievement

At the start of each *Small Changes* programme clients set goals that they wish to achieve. These can be simple, such as lowered cholesterol, a certain amount of exercise per day, weight loss. The essence of *Small Changes* is that the intervention is small. It is this small step that makes the goal reachable. As a client said:

> I think that is what is (particularly) good about the intervention – that you are only changing something small and therefore it seems all of sudden manageable.

Facilitation

A special feature of each project is the use of small learning sets and a supervisor. These elements are crucial in creating the correct environment for the client. In all cases clients wrote about how the course team and the students had created an environment conducive to success. An accolade from one client that encapsulates this said

> I feel the whole environment which Jean and Trevor (the tutors) have created here has been amazing.

Impacts on the students

Impacts on the students have been collected through the quality processes used at Sheffield Hallam to hear the 'voice of the student'. These include quantitative and qualitative data from the module evaluation questionnaires, evidence from course committees, reflective diaries and comments from the external participants. From this evidence three themes emerge: the impact on knowledge and skills acquisition; employability and student satisfaction.

Impact on knowledge and skills

Virtually every student reported that their skills and knowledge had increased as a consequence of the *Small Changes* project. These skills include dealing with the general public as well as practical or professional skills, such as taking the anthropometric measures. Knowledge of the subject matter was increased by the application of theory to practice and having to explain such concepts to members of the public who do not possess the students' mastery or scientific background. One student neatly summed this up when they said,

> learning (about the details of what causes obesity) what it is and (how all the anthropometric measurements work) these other things are, is remarkable and very useful.

Employability

From the employability diaries kept as part of the project assessment, it became obvious that the students valued the skills which they learned and could take with them into employment. Importantly, most of the students mentioned that they had gained in confidence and now felt more able to deal with the world of work. This is an employability attribute that probably cannot be taught, but is sometimes regarded as underpinning most of the other attributes (Nield, 2006).

These changes in perceived level of employability accord with the findings in the section on employers and employment below.

Student satisfaction

From all of the methods used to collect the student data it is apparent that students have been extremely happy with the course, the way that it has been run, and how it has enhanced their learning. This contributed to the 97% overall satisfaction score in the National Student Survey recorded by students studying nutrition, which included the students who took part in this module.

Impacts on the university

The impacts on the department, the school and the university are twofold:

First, the university receives acknowledgment that its presence is beneficial for the local community and although this benefit is difficult to quantify, funding has increased to a research grant of £1.2 million. This money is being used to take the work *Small Changes* is doing on obesity to Barnsley, and this will be on a much larger scale.

Secondly, a further £92,000 has been received by the school to carry out the *Moving Forward* project which uses the *Small Changes* approach to improve key lifestyle behaviours in the region. Students are involved in the collection of data and as assistants on the delivery of training sessions. This work is currently being evaluated with the assistance of final-year students in the school.

Impacts on employers/employment

Since the inception of this project a clear link between the project and employment has emerged. Ex-students from the courses have found employment with the university; for example, two graduates are now working on the new Barnsley project as a direct result of their involvement in *Small Changes*. Another graduate has found full time employment in work of a similar nature as she is part of the Bactive campaign (the project that encompasses the £1.2 million funding mentioned above). Two other ex-students who have worked for *Small Changes* have now taken on academic roles related to food and nutrition in the university.

Conclusion

The programme is meeting its aims of providing students with real-life experience while engaging with the general public. From the evaluation of both students and the general public it would seem that the students are engaged with learning and that the clients (the public) are improving their personal health and wellbeing. It would thus appear that the programme is highly effective. (Simper et al, 2008; 2009)

❏ Students can provide benefits that impact significantly on the general public.
❏ The learning environment (specifically the supervision and educational ethos provided by the learning sets) encourages learning and the further development of knowledge and skills by the students.
❏ Other stakeholders, the university and employers, benefit both directly and indirectly from the work of the students.

The initiative was based on a project module that had been designed to be flexible, to allow staff to design an academically rigorous module that would also meet the needs of the students. As a consequence, the module was able to develop at its own speed and improve as it has matured.

From the employment impact and from the student diaries it can be concluded that the employability skills of the students have been much enhanced by engagement with the project. Two former students from the school who are both now employed on the project commented:

Having worked on Small Changes for two-and-a-half years now, we have a much-improved skill set in nutrition and behaviour change, along with experience of project work and the challenges of working in a deprived community. Experience of working within a specific community means that the courses can be made realistic and relevant to the needs of participants. Working unsupervised, away from the workplace environment, but also as part of a close-knit team, requires the ability to work independently and work well with other people.

Through working on Small Changes we have gained skills in behaviour change and coaching skills, which lead to clients taking control of their own health and well being. They gain confidence in their own abilities to affect change. A number of students have already gone on to take up employment in the same sorts of work. They acknowledge how their employability skills have improved and also, importantly, what they have to do to maintain and improve those skills.

From the evaluations it is apparent that the programme is largely successful and is instrumental in creating graduates who are likely to have impact in this area of endeavour. The learning environment created by the use of small learning sets, and the overall organisation of the course have led to learning that is valued by the students, the general public and prospective employers.

References

Foresight Report (2007) *Tackling Obesities Future Choices*. London: Government Office for Science

Knight, P. and Yorke, M. (2004) *Learning, Curriculum and Employability in Higher Education*. London: Routledge Falmer

Nield, K. (2006) Enhancing hospitality-graduate employability. *The Hospitality Review* 7 (3) July 2006 52–57

Simper, T., Paxman, J. and O'Keeffe, J. (2008) Small-group weight management programme using self-selected goals improves General Well Being scores. *International Journal of Obesity* May S230

Simper, T., O'Keeffe, J., Harden C. and Paxman, J. (2009) Reduced energy intake and maintained loss of weight is observed at 6 months follow up of the 'Small Changes Programme'. *European Journal of Obesity* May 2 (S2) 228

KEVIN NIELD is head of department of Service Sector Management in the Sheffield Business School at Sheffield Hallam University. Before taking up his present position Kevin worked in the catering and retail industries and in further education. He joined Sheffield Hallam in 1990 and has held a variety of positions including programme leader, subject team leader and teaching fellow. He is widely published and has over 70 refereed articles and papers; he has co-researched three editions of the British Hospitality Association's annual *British Hospitality: Trends and Statistics* and is joint author of *Contemporary Issues in Hospitality and Tourism in China and India*. His research interests include international pedagogy and graduate employability

Kevin is an advisory group member of the HE Academy network for Hospitality, Leisure, Sport and Tourism and has represented the sector on QAA working groups and panels. He has been Chair of the Council for Hospitality Management Education's (CHME) Learning and Teaching Group and a member of the Executive Committee. Currently, he is Director of Education for EuroChrie.

TREVOR SIMPER is a senior lecturer/researcher in food and nutrition at Sheffield Hallam University and a registered public health nutritionist. Trevor's undergraduate studies were in health and sport science. He has a masters degree in public health and health promotion from Leeds Metropolitan University and a postgraduate teaching certificate for higher education from Sheffield Hallam. Trevor's current doctoral studies focus on weight management, nutrition, exercise and behaviour.

Trevor co-ordinated the Bradford Food Network for several years which won the Caroline Walker Trust award for improving public health through good food in 2005. He worked for various health promotion departments in the London Borough of Southwark, Staffordshire and Bradford in West Yorkshire before becoming a full time academic. Trevor is now also a director of the social enterprise – Small Changes (Healthcare) Ltd (www.small-changes.co.uk).

13

Using student part-time work for structured and credit-rated work-based learning

Chrissy Ogilvie and Sue Shaw
Manchester Metropolitan University Business School

This chapter describes how student part-time work was used in a university business school as a basis for academic study and credit for first-year undergraduates. With careful management of the total learning environment by the module leader, undertaking this work-based learning module enhanced both the students' understanding of business processes and impacted positively on their performance at work, job satisfaction and employability as graduates.[1]

Objectives

Increasingly, it is an economic necessity for undergraduate students to take part-time work alongside their studies in order to fund their education. At Manchester Metropolitan Business School, this trend was seen as an opportunity to enrich the business curriculum by linking academic theory to real life contexts. Popular media and academic research has tended to focus on the detrimental impact that casual employment has on students' studies and academic performance (Curtis, 2007; Robotham, 2009; Van Dyke et al, 2005).

This case study challenges that view by demonstrating that, if designed and delivered appropriately as part of the formal curriculum, this form of work-based learning (WBL) can have numerous benefits including enhanced graduate employability and work readiness. The WBL modules offer students the opportunity to critically explore organisation and management issues in a live context, thus deepening their engagement with learning. WBL also supports the widening participation agendas by helping students from less advantaged backgrounds who have to work, and students who learn best in non-classroom settings. The blended learning design offers a contrast and an alternative to the more traditional delivery through live lectures and tutorials.

---

1   The authors gratefully acknowledge the permission to use material from their contribution to the *Journal of European Industrial Training* 34 (8/9) 'Making a virtue out of a necessity: part time work as a site for undergraduate work based learning' (2010) 805–21.

Rationale and context

Informal research suggests that between 25 and 35% of full time undergraduate students at Manchester Metropolitan University Business School (MMUBS) have part-time paid work. Using the workplace as an arena for business learning was the rationale behind the design of a series of progressive, yet free-standing, 20-credit elective WBL modules offered to first, second and third-year undergraduate students on a range of business degree programmes. A requirement is that students should undertake 100 hours of work, paid or voluntary, in the period of study. In practice, very few students take the voluntary route even though it offers CV-development benefits. This case study focuses on data from a formal evaluation of the first year (Level 4) WBL module in its inception. Student employment ranges across sectors but includes a proportion working in hospitality (bars and restaurants), leisure and sport (swimming pools, concert arenas, football grounds, beauty spas, night-clubs) and tourism (hotels, holiday parks).

Description

As part of its review of programmes and desire to introduce more student choice into the first and second years of study, MMUBS decided to make a virtue out of the economic necessity for students who work part-time and devise a series of accredited WBL modules based on this casual employment. This type of informal WBL differs from much of the published literature on the subject, which primarily focuses on placements and internships (Brennan, 2005; Brennan and Little, 2006). In the WBL described here, there is no formal relationship between student and employer as with placement or internships. The modules were designed specifically for students who were in employment primarily for financial support; this work could be quite low-level and not necessarily degree-related. An element of their design was to ensure that students could draw on the work experience gained in every size of organisation from corner shop to hotel chain.

The first year WBL module enables students in part-time jobs to explore organisation and management issues in a real context. It starts with an introductory lecture or workshop and is followed by lectures and tutorial support delivered through the virtual learning environment. Assignments are work-based by means of a portfolio which includes a face-to-face presentation and business improvement report. It was also assumed that student employment would be low level and possibly intermittent and therefore not conducive to project work. The unit content therefore focused on generic organisational behaviour topics such as stakeholders, structure, culture, communication and health and safety as well as broader business issues of quality, corporate social responsibility (CSR) and waste management.

While this form of WBL fits broadly into Seagraves et al's idea of 'learning *through* work' (1996), it differs from most conceptualisations of WBL (Boud et al, 2001; Smith and Betts, 2000) in that it specifically requires no formal partnership between the university and employer. The only contract that exists therefore is a standard employment contact or voluntary-work agreement, which does not cover or refer to this form of learning. This means that there is no relationship between the university and the 'employer' (used in its widest sense to cover any of the forms of work outlined above) and no formal role or obligation to participate.

The employer or line manager is not required to support or facilitate the academic learning of the student in the workplace. Employer support, a key variable for student success in WBL is therefore not under the control of the university. Students are encouraged to mobilise the support of their employer for their studies and are given support in this process. However, students with long-standing work relationships with managers find workplace research and learning easier than others who have less 'relationship capital' and may experience hard-pressed or even defensive managers who fear students may be judging and criticising their performance.

While the main aims of the module were to provide students with an opportunity to learn in a different way from that of the conventional classroom by linking business theory with actual practice, it also offered flexible delivery, being on-line. This was appreciated by students who are already balancing work with academic commitments and who increasingly seem to live at home and travel into the university from a distance.

Evaluation

The formal evaluation conducted in 2008–9 revealed many positive benefits for all stakeholders; students, tutors, university and employers. Satisfaction levels among students taking this unit were high. In the first year evaluation, the overriding benefit reported by half of the cohort was flexibility in delivery.

> The flexibility to do your work when you have time gives you a healthy work/study balance. To be able to have the flexibility and not a rushed approach has made me take more interest in this module and help me gain the grades I have.

This flexibility was perceived as no obligation to attend lessons, fewer timetabling restrictions, anytime access to on-line materials, less travel, freedom to work from home, combining study with earning, freedom to study in their own time and at their own pace, anytime email access to tutors, and the freedom to organise oneself, being 'more like the real world'. Just two students felt that lack of direct contact with tutors and fellow students had an adverse effect on their academic performance.

In addition to giving them academic credit, there was strong evidence that doing the module impacted positively on the students' performance at work and job satisfaction. For example:

> I really do enjoy my job, at first I wasn't too interested about work and when I got home I would just switch off, but by understanding the company more in-depth I like going to work more.

What I liked about this unit is that I get good ideas which I take into work and get the credit for them.

There was also evidence that WBL extended on-the-job training opportunities for some students and opened new directions for further study. Ambitious students used WBL as a way of getting themselves known by their employers with a view to long-term graduate employment:

Managers take you more seriously because you show interest – you're more valued.

I have enjoyed the extra responsibilities being given to me, such as being the organiser of the main Easter event at (a major supermarket chain)... I think my manager feels she has benefited from me doing this module as I have been able to bring more of my knowledge to the business and therefore do a better job.

Apart from more motivated employees, there were other benefits for employers such as business development, vicarious management development and graduate recruitment. One student sent his report to the CEO of his company and received a positive response. Another wrote:

After presenting these ideas to my manager, she also found they would help the company and will be briefing them ... in her next team meeting with the company management.

Significant evidence also emerged as to the perceived value of the place of employment as an arena for learning and putting theory into practice:

I see my workplace as a business now. Just like when I did media studies it changed the way I watched television programmes, WBL has changed how I look at my work.

Strong evidence emerged as to the perceived value of the place of employment as an arena for learning and putting theory into practice. Two-thirds of students gave 'theory into practice' as the prime reason for their choice of this module. Seeing how 'classroom concepts' could be translated into a business was key to the quality of the learning experience for almost all students.

They also learned more about the organisation they worked for:

This module has made me feel more integrated into my workplace now I know how everything works and why certain rules are in place.

and with that had come greater understanding:

I now understand and respect how hard it is for an organisation to run smoothly. Things that used to cause a problem for me do not any more, as I have seen the grand scheme of things.'

Seeing how 'classroom concepts' could be translated into a business was key to the quality of the learning experience for almost all students. Certainly, working students are less naïve in their understanding of management issues than those without employment experience. It may be that this form of WBL favours the active and pragmatic learners who in one study reported that they disliked sitting passively and found lectures 'boring' (Honey & Mumford, 1992). Much business-school learning delivery favours theorists and reflectors so this approach can be seen as mitigating that tendency. It could also be argued that activist learning strongly features in the informal learning of working managers and therefore developing this learning style in all students enhances future graduate performance. The unit may also have raised aspirations:

> ..it made me think I would love to be in a managerial role, as it is very challenging.

In their reflections, some students recognised that the blended learning style had fostered skills of independence and confidence.

> I have learnt that I can work through problems on my own and it has helped me to work independently at my own pace and not to doubt myself so much.
>
> it forces you to learn off your own back which is a valuable skill when in university.

The module required self-discipline and students needed to become proactive in seeking support from tutors and fellow students. Those who did email tutors were very pleased that they received prompt and helpful responses. However, not all students rose to this challenge, falling behind in both weekly online tutorials and with deadlines. The seven students who submitted re-sit work had failed because they had missed some assignments and three had submitted no work at all. A few said that they missed social interaction, even though their other five modules were classroom-based. More research is planned to identify the learning preferences of those students who continued to choose this elective in subsequent years.

Students also learned about themselves and their capabilities as well as skills of reflection:

> This module has been a massive eye-opener into what materials and technology I need [as an employee] yet seemed to blank over. I have now established that I am a laid-back learner with the ability to learn more greatly if I just open my mind a little and analyse each aspect in more detail.

The learning process of WBL therefore stretches students in terms of researching in the workplace, mobilising their employer's support in their studies, contextualising theory and being proactive and independent in their studies. It also helps students become consciously aware of their informal learning at work. The CareerEDGE model of graduate employment (Dacre Pool and Sewell, 2007: see Figure 1) suggests that a process of reflection and evaluation on key inputs of experience and learning help to build self-efficacy, self-confidence and self-esteem which lead to employability. One of the five inputs is experience of work and life, which in WBL links explicitly with the degree content. This link will be less strong with students on non-business degrees unless their casual employment links to their chosen vocation, but the broader benefits of WBL in terms of employability and impact in graduate jobs will still accrue.

The weekly online tutorials invite the students to answer reflective and evaluative

The CareerEDGE Model of Graduate Employability

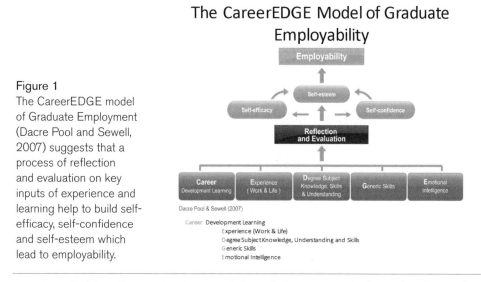

Figure 1

The CareerEDGE model of Graduate Employment (Dacre Pool and Sewell, 2007) suggests that a process of reflection and evaluation on key inputs of experience and learning help to build self-efficacy, self-confidence and self-esteem which lead to employability.

questions linking the academic material to their own workplace. A prime role of the tutor is to help students who struggle to contextualise the learning, particularly in small, less formal, employing organisations. There is evidence that student self-esteem and confidence is enhanced through the process, especially when they fed back their observations to their employer and found appreciation and even acceptance. Moreover, when presenting their work to tutors, the students take on the mantle of 'expert' on their organisation, acting as a 'company employee' as well as a student. Finally the process of becoming an independent learner who can view any level of employment as a site for learning can be seen as developing self-efficacy.

The delivery of the module also provides informal learning for tutors who gain insight through engaging with students and marking assignments into the realities of the current workplace in a range of contexts and operational levels. Not only are assignments interesting and informative to mark, the issues they raise enriches the development of the curriculum.

Main learning points

From our own experiences and reflections on its operation, for the module to be fully effective, careful attention needs to be paid to the students' learning experience in its totality (Shaw and Ogilvie, 2010). This means addressing not just the formal cognitive-based student learning but also the non-formal and informal learning which is grounded in experience, enquiry and reflection arising from their motivation and autonomy.

With a form of learning where the tutors have no control over a substantial part of the learning environment, particular care needs to be taken to engineer and indeed simulate aspects of work-based learning that cannot be guaranteed in the context where the students are operating. This includes not just the social aspects of learning, but also the more general learning factors such as feedback, challenge and support for learning. Tutors also need to be mindful that this kind of approach may appeal more strongly to active and pragmatic learners, and consequently need to establish additional support mechanisms for these learners to better develop their theorising and reflective skills.

In terms of helping students attain graduate employment and producing graduates who are equipped to make an impact this form of WBL contributes in a number of ways. The innovative nature of the module certainly provides a contrasting mode of unit delivery and learning experience for the traditional undergraduate student and this might be one that has appeal to current students who, as members of Generation Y or the 'millennial generation' are seen to have an individualistic approach and prefer more personalised work (Sayers, 2007). Moreover, given the current (2011) debate about funding in the HE sector and the imminent lifting of the cap on student fees, it could be argued that the chapter shows how this type of accredited WBL can deliver a range of student benefits and could be adopted more widely.

Such an experience not only deepens students' learning about business but also equips them to contribute very early on in their graduate careers. It creates a greater awareness and deepened understanding of the operational realities of working life. Furthermore, it enhances employability through developing skills in such areas as handling relationships and self-directed learning. Self-directed and informal learning raises the student's profile in part-time work and may open up immediate or longer-term job prospects, facilitating graduate entry to employment by adding value to low-level work experience.

WBL can also be seen to build student confidence, self-esteem and self-efficacy in line with Dacre Pool & Sewell's CareerEDGE model (2007) above. Although this was originally designed specifically for business-degree programmes, there are now moves in the university to design 15 credit-elective WBL units for all second and third-year undergraduates in part-time work, as a way of enhancing employability.

As we enter a tighter economic climate and more challenging job market, universities may seek further opportunities to help their students be more employable and have a more immediate impact in their graduate employment destination by capitalising on their part-time work as undergraduates. This case study demonstrates one way this can be achieved.

References and URLs

Boud, D., Solomon, N. and Symes, C. (2001) New Practices for New Times. In Boud, D. and Solomon, N. (eds) *Work Based Learning: A New Higher Education?* Buckingham: The Society for Research into Higher Education & Open University Press pp 3–17

Brennan, L. (2005) Integrating Work-based Learning into Higher Education – A Guide to Good Practice. Bolton: University Vocational Awards Council

Brennan, J and Little, B. (2006) Towards a Strategy for Workplace Learning: report of a study to assist HEFCE in the development of a strategy for workplace learning. London: Centre for Higher

Education Research & Information

Curtis, S. (2007) Student Perceptions of the Effects of Term-time Paid Employment. *Education & Training* 49 (5) 380–90

Dacre Pool, L. and Sewell, P. (2007) The key to employability: developing a practical model of graduate employability *Education & Training* 49 (4) 277–89

Honey, P. and Mumford, A. (1992) *Manual of Learning Styles* 3rd edn. London: Peter Honey

Robotham, D. (2009) Combining study and employment: a step too far?' *Education & Training* 51 (4) 322–32

Sayers, R. (2007) The right staff from X to Y. *Library Management* 28 (8/9) 474–87

Seagraves, I., Osborne, M., Neal, P., Dockrell, R., Hartshorn, C. and Boyd, A. (1996) *Learning in Smaller Companies (LISC) Final Report*. University of Stirling: Educational Policy and Development.

Shaw, S and Ogilvie, C. (2010) Making a virtue out of a necessity: part time work as a site for undergraduate work based learning. *Journal of European Industrial Training* 34 (8/9) 805–21

Smith, R and Betts, M. (2000) Learning as Partners: realising the potential of work-based learning. *Journal of Vocational Education and Training* 52 (4) 589–604

Van Dyke, R., Little, B. and Callender, C. (2005) *Survey of students' attitudes to debt and term-time working and their impact on attainment*. At www.hefce.ac.uk/pubs/rdreports. Accessed September 4, 2009

CHRISSY OGILVIE is a senior lecturer in management at Manchester Metropolitan University Business School. Her main responsibilities are work-based learning, which runs at every level in undergraduate programmes and in postgraduate degree and certificate awards. She is also integrating management awards validated by the Chartered Management Institute into work-based learning and other business degree modules. Her current research interests are also in work-based learning.

SUE SHAW is head of the Human Resource Management & Organisational Behaviour Division at MMUBS. Her teaching and research interests are in international HRM/HRD, individual performance and women in management. She has produced a number of publications and conference papers in these areas. She is currently leading the School's four year METP EU/China management development project. Sue is a chartered fellow of Chartered Institute of Personnel and Development (CIPD) and has been actively engaged with the CIPD for a number of years, locally, nationally and internationally.

14

Developing professional values and behaviour in a virtual learning environment

Karen Barton and Fiona Westwood
University of Strathclyde

When law students are able to gain valuable experience about how they will be expected to work in professional practice, they can develop the skills to act as graduates with impact. Using an online simulated learning environment to create team-based projects and close working relationships with experienced tutor practitioners, it is possible to influence the development of professional values and behaviour.

Context and rationale

This chapter is based on the experiences of approximately 200 postgraduate students completing the Diploma in Legal Practice (DLP) at the Centre for Professional Legal Studies, the Law School, University of Strathclyde (CPLS). After completing their undergraduate law degree, students who wish to become practising solicitors attend for one academic year and take the DLP required by the Law Society of Scotland (LSS) prior to entry to the next stage of their formal training, the two-year traineeship. The LSS prescribes the content of the DLP which is heavily based on vocational skill development and enables students to make the transition to trainee practitioners.

There is considerable competition for traineeships, with an oversupply of applicants, so it is essential that students are able to show that they have the knowledge, skills and professional attitude needed to be of value to potential employers. Employers vary from large commercially orientated law firms, through to government bodies and small local practices, with the result that students have to demonstrate that they understand the core requirements of professional legal practice and that their skill development is transferable.

Employers want employees to adopt a positive attitude to learning.

> What individuals know on their own is less important than what they can do with others to 'add value' to the enterprise; learning becomes collaborative, outward looking and goal oriented rather than an end in itself (Boon et al, 2005: 481).

To do this, they have to take personal responsibility for their own learning by

> (adopting) a series of behaviours which enables an individual to structure and motivate his or her work behaviour by setting goals, practising new and desired

behaviours, keeping track of progress and rewarding himself or herself for goal achievement (van der Sluis and Lidway, 2002: 21).

Team working, employability and safe environments

More and more emphasis is being placed by employers on graduates being able to work in professional teams where people act with integrity and are committed to a high quality service for clients and support colleagues. To improve the vocational skills element of the course, a virtual-learning environment (VLE) has been developed at CPLS with students working in groups of four in virtual law firms, completing a series of legal transactions with formative and summative assessment based on their 'firm' performance. Students do not select who they work with but instead are allocated groups at random. While regarded as a 'safe' learning environment for the students, in that they are not exposed to working with real clients, the reality is that student learning is determined by the success of the dynamics in their group.

Given the short duration of the course, they have limited time before undertaking their client projects, to get to know each other and gain an appreciation of individual abilities and styles of working. Some firms develop mutual trust and act with personal and professional integrity, others do not. Their tutors often perceive tensions between the various values and behaviours of individual members of each firm and want to be able to intervene and resolve these. As Fiona had overall responsibility for developing the students into trainee practitioners, and Karen for the effectiveness of the VLE as an integral learning tool, they discussed how best to improve the individual student's experience and tutors' resources to tackle overtly the negative aspects of the group dynamics. They agreed that both students and tutors needed to be provided with both hard and soft support to address these issues so as to accelerate the learning and professional development achieved.

One particular source of information detailing the student experience is contained in the individual reflective reports that are the required assessed piece of work for the compulsory *Practice Management* (PM) module. It was decided to analyse these reports in detail over a three-year period, and a matrix was developed to assess the trust and learning of individual firms. This demonstrated that initially only about 25% of firms achieved high levels of both. As a result, it was decided that active interventions had to be taken to improve the experience of learning and trust for every firm.

The matrix that was developed (see Figure 1) to explain the results of the analysis identified four types of firm:

- ❏ Learning communities   (high trust and high learning)
- ❏ Legal eagles   (low trust and high learning)
- ❏ Happy families   (high trust and low learning)
- ❏ Dysfunctional   (low trust and low learning)

The analysis of firms examined their culture, approach to tasks, relationships and work styles.

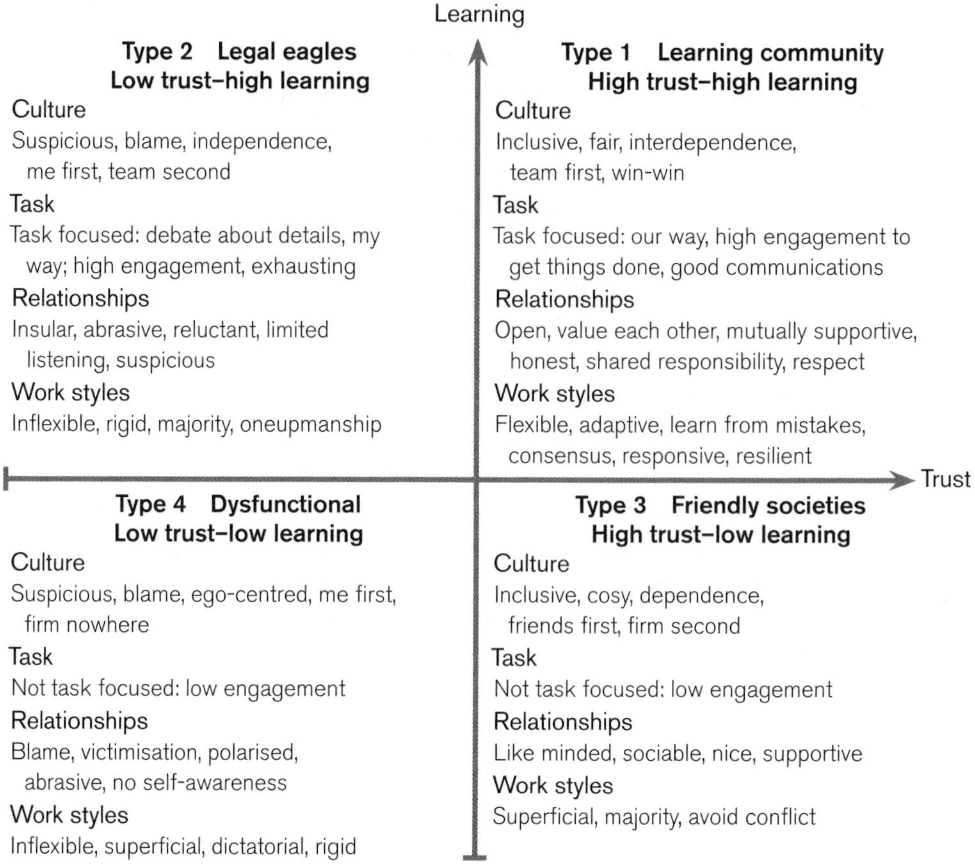

Learning

Type 2   Legal eagles
Low trust–high learning

Culture

Suspicious, blame, independence,
  me first, team second

Task

Task focused: debate about details, my
  way; high engagement, exhausting

Relationships

Insular, abrasive, reluctant, limited
  listening, suspicious

Work styles

Inflexible, rigid, majority, oneupmanship

Type 1   Learning community
High trust–high learning

Culture

Inclusive, fair, interdependence,
  team first, win-win

Task

Task focused: our way, high engagement to
  get things done, good communications

Relationships

Open, value each other, mutually supportive,
  honest, shared responsibility, respect

Work styles

Flexible, adaptive, learn from mistakes,
  consensus, responsive, resilient

Trust

Type 4   Dysfunctional
Low trust–low learning

Culture

Suspicious, blame, ego-centred, me first,
  firm nowhere

Task

Not task focused: low engagement

Relationships

Blame, victimisation, polarised,
  abrasive, no self-awareness

Work styles

Inflexible, superficial, dictatorial, rigid

Type 3   Friendly societies
High trust–low learning

Culture

Inclusive, cosy, dependence,
  friends first, firm second

Task

Not task focused: low engagement

Relationships

Like minded, sociable, nice, supportive

Work styles

Superficial, majority, avoid conflict

Figure 1 The learning/trust matrix
Source: Barton & Westwood (2006)

Figure 1 shows that the firms which performed well – the Learning communities – adopted an inclusive culture that focused on the task in hand, communicated well with each other and adapted their style of working to suit the particular project they were working on. Legal eagles, while they were also highly task-focused, exhausted everyone by being argumentative and abrasive with each other in the process of getting the job done. They had to be encouraged by their tutors to learn to trust each other. On the other hand, happy families were not task focused and did not take their group work seriously. As a result, their tutors had to facilitate their engagement and learning. The Dysfunctional firms were very difficult to tackle and took up considerable amount of time and effort on the part of their tutors who found it difficult to formalise their group discussions and keep them objective.

Providing both hard and soft support

The PM course is taught by legal practitioners employed as tutors, with the assigned role of 'practice manager' to their student firm. This formal role encompasses responsibility for the overall performance of the firm, through mentoring, in relation to project delivery and client service. While the student learning activities per se take place in these virtual firms, the tutors meet on a regular basis with individual student firms. All PM tutors are selected on the basis of their people development abilities rather than their legal expertise and are given training in enhancing their 'coaching' skills. In addition, the VLE provides each firm with an intranet, activity logs, peer assessment tools and reflective logs which can be accessed confidentially by the tutor and individual student.

At the first meeting with the PM tutor, the matrix is explained to the students including the characteristics of the four types. Each firm is asked to identify and agree core values for the firm as whole and specific exercises are included to allow individuals to discuss their preferences in relation to styles of working, other commitments and communications. They are provided with a template for a written Partnership Agreement and required to complete and formally sign this within four weeks of the start of the DLP.

Enabling factors

What enables this practice to work is the blending of hard and soft support. Hard support, such as formal feedback, peer assessment and reflective logs, allows both students and teachers to discuss factual performance rather than purely 'emotive' examples, such as 'not liking' the other student. The formality of signing a legal document in the form of a contract has particular significance for law students as it requires them to articulate and address individual concerns at an early stage rather than leave them 'under the surface' of their relationships. The use of core values, an important part of professional dynamics, helps to agree a frame of reference for everyone to work within. It also allows the teacher to refer to what was written there if later problems develop. Students start to use the names of the four types to better explain to each other when tensions or behavioural problems arise.

Evaluation of its effectiveness and appropriateness

Analysis of the reflective reports was carried out in the year following the introduction of these interventions and it was possible to plot a statistical improvement in the percentage of the firms in the high trust and high learning quadrant. This allowed us to demonstrate that the enabling factors had intervened successfully in encouraging the Legal eagle firms to move beyond their initial lack of trust and get on with the tasks more collectively. The Friendly societies were able to focus much more on their learning, rather than on being 'nice' to each other. Individual students in the Dysfunctional firms gained more confidence in expressing their concerns, allowing the tutors to address more of the core issues rather than spending time on noisy distractions. In general, potentially Dysfunctional firms were picked up on earlier and targeted specialist support such as formal mediation, was offered in an attempt to openly resolve the underlying issues. Overall, the tutors felt able to contribute positively to enhancing the reality of professional practice experiences.

Impact

Being aware of the increased pressures on student employability, we obtained employer comments on what they see as the value of the students' experience of working in these virtual firms. Despite the inherent emphasis of linking individual success to individual performance at undergraduate level, employers want graduates who are able to work effectively with other people, sharing knowledge and expertise so to allow the organisation as a whole to perform well.

Learning from and working with colleagues is an important part of becoming a practising professional, as it teaches

> behaviours such as listening and constructively responding to points of view expressed by others, giving others the benefit of the doubt, providing support to those who need it and recognising the interests and achievements of others (Katzenbach and Smith, 1993: 21).

Employers

As a result, employers said that, for the vast majority, the opportunity to work in a virtual firm and build relationships with other people – in particular to learn what it is like to work well under stress – is of considerable advantage to the students, and gives them an excellent start to their traineeship. Of particular importance are:

❏ being able to deal with prioritising multiple tasks
❏ experience of working collectively to deadlines
❏ working with different people and different personalities
❏ being able to interact with other team members and take responsibility for work within a team
❏ feeling more comfortable with being able to delegate tasks
❏ giving the student a taste of what it is like to work in a real firm.

One employer comment illustrates the latter point:

> From a purely practical point of view, I think the students benefit from working on basic non-legal administrative tasks which might seem mundane when they are being experienced during the course of the DLP but which are every day occurrences when they are carrying out their traineeship.

Students

Students' comments mirror these views. They speak of becoming more comfortable with working with other people, of appreciating the demands of working to deadlines and of accepting that tensions will arise. For example,

- It has taught me to put more faith in other people and to realise that working with others and sharing responsibility can be a very valuable way of working. … it has taught me that working with others can lead to learning a lot more, and however confident you are about your own abilities, it is often important and helpful to have another point of view.

- Delegation of the work became second nature as we grew in confidence that the other members of the group were just as reliable as ourselves. We all shared the same desire to 'get the projects done' and at the same time didn't want to let our friends down.

- I had to learn to take a step back and accept that everyone had different methods of working and that although mine suited me, it did not necessarily suit everyone. Another aspect that I found challenging was the trust that was required between members of the firm…. You required to trust in the capabilities of other members of the group.

- Personally I really feel the firm has worked well together. It has such a mix of characters all with different idea of how something should be done. At the start I was worried because everybody seemed to want to lead and this normally poses conflict. This never happened and firm members were often quite frank with one another but this was always done in the right manner.

- The main thing is that we respected and listened to each other. The firm was continually supportive to each other and was always willing to take on a larger share of the workload, should somebody else have other commitments or course work to do. Each person brought their own strengths to the group and we chose to use this to the firm's advantage.

- A time-management issue which I think caused friction with some of the other members was my time keeping skills… I appreciate that this must have been very annoying for others… However, I worked hard to ensure that the others did not have to do my share of the work as a result of my lateness… Taught me invaluable lessons regarding firm dynamics and administration.

- Before working in the firm, I had the perception that I was not an ideas person and much happier following than leading. Now I feel that I can lead a project and be an active member of a team. Being in a firm is a great way to make friends on the diploma and has prepared me for dealing with future colleagues.

- Working within the firm has allowed us to really get to know each other, to trust one another and to work effectively together. It has not been an easy road and there have been occasions where disagreements have been encountered. We have, however, learned to deal with such situations and move forward. I think it was important that things did not always run smoothly because in reality things will not and you have to be able to adapt to and deal with such situations.

- Generally I felt that it was better to deal with problems rather than to dwell on difficulties. This enabled us to delegate tasks more effectively and ensured that we met all our deadlines....essentially all members have to learn to compromise.

Barriers and challenges

One challenge was to recruit tutors who were skilled at recognising each firm's dynamics and intervening when appropriate. Experienced practitioners are not always able to make the tacit explicit and can find it difficult to articulate unspoken elements of professional values and behaviours. As a result, it was important to select tutors who had the ability to be good teachers, support them through training and provide them with formal structuring tools.

Another barrier that needed to be addressed was students' reluctance to accept assessment of the team's performance rather than their own. Their undergraduate experience had allowed them to set and work to their own deadlines and work standards, and their success was therefore personal to them. In some cases, they had also had a negative experience of 'team working,' with the result that they came to the VLE projects with a suspicious or even negative orientation. It was important to address this at the outset through an explanation of the matrix and the discussions they had before formalising their written partnership agreement.

Lessons learned we recommend to colleagues

❑ Simulated learning environments offer considerable potential to assist students in experiencing the realities of professional practice.

❑ The ability to work in teams by demonstrating professional values and behaviours is an essential aspect of future employability.

❑ It is important not to assume that simulations are 'safe' in relation to the students' experience with the result that skilled teachers are needed to facilitate their learning.

❑ The student experience in the simulated virtual learning environment is not without risks of real inter-personal problems. It is important to provide students and skilled teachers with formal processes that allow them to articulate and address concerns about personal integrity, core values and unprofessional behaviour.

❑ Our own learning was based on our acceptance that the VLE mirrored the challenges of professional practice where tensions can run high when people are faced with coping with competing demands, time pressures and different styles of working. It was essential, rather than try to belittle or ignore these issues, leaving it for the students to work through themselves, to deliver specific interventions. We felt that these had to include upskilling our tutors as well as providing them with formal tools to structure and facilitate development of both each student's professional working skills and their professional character.

Conclusions

Given current pressures on universities to enhance employability, we feel that the experience of working in virtual teams allows students an insight into what will be expected of them when they make the transition to the workplace. It therefore enables them to shift somewhat from their undergraduate level approach to learning and individual performance, to the skills and attitudes that are essential for a sustainable successful career. Formalising the learning and trust of simulated high performing teams encourages students to recognise the essential nature of these and apply them in real life work with their colleagues and clients.

References

Barton, K. & Westwood, F. 2006. From student to trainee practitioner – a study of team working as a learning experience. *Web Journal of Current Legal Issues.* **3** http://webjcli.ncl.ac.uk/2006/issue3/barton-westwood3.html

Boon, A., Flood, J. & Webb, J. 2005. Postmodern Professions? The fragmentation of legal education and the legal profession. *Journal of Law and Society* **32** (3) September 473–92

Katzenbach, J. R. & Smith, D. K. 1993. *The wisdom of teams – creating the high performance organisation.* Boston: Harvard Business School Press

van der Sluis & Lideway (2002) Learning behaviour and learning opportunities as career stimuli. *Journal of Workplace Learning* **14** (1/2) 19-30

KAREN BARTON is co-director of professional practice courses at the University of Strathclyde Law School. With a long-term interest in professional learning, she has carried out a number of funded research projects in these areas, including the Standardised Client Initiative in interviewing skills; an investigation on the use of e-portfolios in professional legal education; and an Open Educational Resources project on simulations, SimShare. She is currently a member of the university's cross-disciplinary research group in Professionalism and Professional Learning; an active participant in national and international conferences; and author of a number of articles and book chapters in these areas.

FIONA WESTWOOD worked in private practice as a solicitor until 1994, latterly as an equity partner in a large law firm, with particular responsibility for business development and training. Since 2000 she has been involved in legal education as tutor and senior lecturer in legal practice at the University of Strathclyde. Her academic publications relate to professionalism, team working and reflective practice and her most recent book, *Developing Resilience – the key to professional success* focuses on personal development. She has presented her research at international conferences, including Ottawa Medical Education 'Assessing Competence' in May 2010.

15

Enhancing graduate skills for a knowledge-based economy
Collaborating with information specialists

Diane Rushton, Alison Lahlafi and Erica Stretton
Sheffield Business School, Sheffield Hallam University

This chapter reflects on a collaboration with information specialists at Sheffield Hallam University to embed graduate attribute research skills into a Year Two (Level 5) module. It discusses the growing importance of information literacy skills within a knowledge-based economy, and how student research skills were developed using a range of assessed and non-assessed module activities.

Rationale and context

Sheffield Hallam University's (SHU) graduate attributes refer to SHU graduates being equipped for 'learning and working in the digital age' (Sheffield Hallam University, 2010). However, although students today are often considered to be of the 'net generation' (Oblinger and Oblinger, 2005: 1–2) and IT literate, tutors at SHU have found that students' ability to use the internet as an effective research tool is overwhelmingly poor. JISC has identified that:

> The internet is the first port of call for information: sites such as Google and Wikipedia are typically referred to before academically approved resources (JISC, 2009: 24).

This correlates with the experience of module tutors teaching the undergraduate Year Two (Level 5) modules, *Managing in a Global Context* (full-time degree/HND) and *Globalisation and Business* (part-time degree) who have found students to have poor information literacy skills, being over-reliant on Google and Wikipedia as reference sources.

As far back as 1993, Drucker spoke of the importance of information literacy skills in the workplace for the survival of business:

> In today's organisation, you have to take responsibility for information because it is your main tool. But most don't know how to use it (Harris, 1993: 120).

A more recent survey of UK SMEs mirrors Drucker's comment that although employees are technologically skilled, they lack information literacy skills (De Saulles, 2007). It reported that although SMEs regard the internet as the single most important source for commercially valuable information, £3.7m annually is spent on time wasted looking for information that they cannot find, and this is a conservative estimate.

There is growing evidence of the importance of information literacy skills to employers. Cheuk concludes that businesses require employees who are 'confident and competent in interacting with information to deliver maximum business value' (2008: 137). Ali and Katz's research into the ICT skills needed by US employers makes the link between the integration of information literacy skills into the business school curriculum and the needs of the workplace, 'essential to provide the business school's graduates with an education fit for the emerging information-centric workplace' (2010: 1).

At module review in 2007–08, recognising the need to improve academic and employability skills and create graduates with impact in a knowledge-based economy, the tutors agreed to proactively address information literacy/research skills in the two Year Two (Level 5) modules, and approached Learning and Information Services (LIS) staff to discuss how we could build on the basic level skills LIS staff had taught these students in Year One (Level 4).

Objectives

The main objectives of the collaboration were:

❏ To further develop students' basic information literacy skills to become independent and discerning users of information in their studies, placement and graduate employment.
❏ To enhance students' research skills in order to further develop their understanding of international business concepts and theories and thereby produce better assignments.
❏ To promote effective use of high-cost electronic databases provided by the university.
❏ To better equip students to cope with the level of research required in their final year and enable them to achieve more highly with this work.

Description

The emphasis of the information-literacy-skills development was on critically analysing, selecting and using business information on the web. It aimed to tackle the 'techno-savvy overconfidence' (Brown et al, 2003: 386) some students display, which they confuse with effective research skills.

Over three years, the collaboration has developed, evolved and embedded a set of assessed and non-assessed learning activities into the modules. These included:

❏ development of a web-based research assessment
❏ assessed reflection on their research skills
❏ joint delivery of interactive lectures
❏ practical computer-based workshops.

Students were able to progress their practical online research skills, applicable to lifelong learners in a knowledge-based economy. They said

> Using the databases more, not going straight to Google.

and

> I had previously avoided using a journal before, possibly due to their size, complexity and the language style used. So this assignment is just what I needed to really move this research method forward and fully widen my approach.

The assessment for the module consisted of three assignments and was designed to enable students to develop specific transferable skills while increasing their subject knowledge. This description gives further detail of how we implemented embedded activities and assessment into the module to improve students' research skills.

The assessment activities and assessment criteria were developed together to achieve the module objectives. The assessment criteria for all pieces of work were the same to ensure that students could see their research skills developing. (See appendix for research-skills assessment criteria). This would allow feedback–'feedforward' (Rushton et al, 2010) from formative assessment into the summative assessment.

The three assignments are interlinked (see Appendix 1 for details of assignments and assessment criteria). The summative assignment is a 5,000-word report, and successful outcome is dependent on the capability to research effectively. This links from the first formative assignment, which was developed to enable students to assess and enhance their current level of research skills while using a wide range of different sources.

In the first assignment the students were required to research the topic of globalisation using five different sources (see Appendix 1). This topic was deliberately broad so that students would have to carefully consider how to refine it. Students then evaluated these sources against the following criteria:

❏ accuracy
❏ authority
❏ objectivity
❏ currency
❏ coverage.

The second part of this assignment was to write a reflective piece on their own research skills, and the use of the internet/online information as a research source.

To assist students in developing the skills needed for their first assignment, the introductory session to the module was jointly delivered by LIS staff and the module leader. At the beginning of this session students were briefed on their first assignment, which then gave context and validity to the remainder of the session delivered by the information specialist.

The emphasis of the session was on creating an interactive experience for students, using a number of activities including demonstrations, discussion, group work and audiovisual material in order to involve the class and build on their prior knowledge.

They were involved in paired and group work focused on identifying the sources they already used, looking at new and alternative business sources, reviewing the pros and cons of newspapers, peer-reviewed journals and Wikipedia. There was some particularly lively debate around the pros and cons of Wikipedia. Demonstrations were given to illustrate the advantages and disadvantages of web resources, and a website evaluation checklist was provided to support an activity where students evaluated Google findings for a search on 'GATT'. Feedback showed that the students regarded this as a worthwhile session:

> I thought the session was really useful – not really used academic journal articles in depth, but I know how to now!

and

> Very informative presentation which I found very useful and feel it will help in future work.

This was followed by further joint input into the second and third assignments (see appendix 1 for details of assignments). A two-hour interactive workshop gave students guidance on accessing relevant databases and other web sources. To ensure relevance and focus to the activities, students were required to research an emerging market and produce a poster for sharing with the class. As a result of student feedback, this was modified to an emerging market relevant to the industry sector of their assignment.

Student feedback indicated they wanted more time in a supportive environment to explore the internet as a research tool and develop their skills. So in the following year this was developed into three computer-laboratory sessions, one information-skills session where students found information which they then developed into a poster in the next two sessions. Further recent initiatives have included researching of copyright-free images and students producing digital posters rather than print posters.

Evaluation and discussion

As the collaboration has progressed, tutors have found that, compared with previous years, the breadth and depth of the sources used is very much improved in the students' final piece of work, the 5,000-word report. LIS staff have also observed students' research skills progressing, for example, broadening use of sources by registering to use databases they had not accessed before.

Although no quantitative data has been collected, there is qualitative data to support the evidence of the effectiveness and appropriateness of this approach to enhance students' research skills, 'Thank you for a very useful session. Before you started I didn't know what a peer-reviewed journal was.' In their self-reflection students commented that they valued this learning opportunity and would have appreciated it in their first year (Level 4). Some recognised that the quality of their work over previous semesters would have been much better if this specific input and support had been given earlier.

Others commented that they had not understood the weaknesses of Wikipedia and Google and not heard of Google Scholar

> finding new sources of information such as Business Source Premier that I had not previously used and which I may therefore use in the future.

It was clear to students that this was a skill that would be transferable across their subject programme,

> I learnt how to make the most from using LitSearch which will help in any module coursework,

in employment or placement.

> I thought the session was good and very informative. In the past I have needed to do a lot of research on packaging and have had to rely on Google!

Student feedback and reflection showed that students saw the value of, and engaged with the activities, especially being given hands-on experience in a supportive environment, 'actively researching with help and understanding available'. This was facilitated by embedding the learning about research in the module and then linking that learning to assessed assignments.

Main learning points

From our experience, consideration needs to be given to the following:

A happy collaboration – how?

Collaboration with colleagues across the university allows for use of different skills and expertise. This collaborative approach has had to meet the needs of both LIS staff and academics, in terms of time, workloads, commitment and transferability. There has to be shared belief in the value of the project outcomes.

In any new initiative the module leader has to secure commitment from the module team. There are issues involved in this holistic pedagogic approach; in particular, the squeezing of precious time from module content can be contentious. There were initial concerns from the module tutors that focusing on research skills detracted from the module content

> I believe more work on explicit connectivity between research skills and module content would be well worthwhile.

The joint sessions need to be managed carefully as students have found it confusing when the sessions led by LIS staff were not sufficiently contextualised by academic tutors:

> I got confused about what we was (sic) doing today compared to the assignment.

Time management

Although initially this concept was developed in revalidation (when it is to be expected that module leaders devote time to develop modules) extra time was, and still is, required for designing and tailoring innovative and collaborative approaches to teaching. Materials and session activities need to be developed and improved over time in response to student feedback and our own reflection.

Student engagement
Some students were reluctant to engage in the process; they considered themselves excellent researchers as they had not received explicit feedback on their research skills before.

> Identifying sources of information for I already know about these, i.e. Euromonitor, Business Source Premier. I used these last year and already know how to use them.

This meant they had to be convinced of the value of the research sessions especially when they could not see how the research activity linked into their assignment. They struggled to see that the activity was a different way of exploring a topic, rather than a standard case-study approach. Therefore, after the first year of this project, the integration between the research activity and the assessment was made more explicit. It was very important to ensure students understand the purpose of the activities is to enhance their academic and employability skills.

Conclusion
The key to success for this project was the commitment of staff involved. The information specialists saw evidence of students developing information literacy skills and maximising the use of high-cost quality online resources provided by SHU. The module leader saw benefits from students enhancing their research skills and thus producing better assignments, eventually leading to higher degree classifications, increasingly demanded by employers, '78% of employers now insist on minimum 2.1 degree' (Association of Graduate Recruiters, 2010). The research skills gained by students will allow them to achieve higher degree classifications and therefore be more attractive to employers looking for high calibre graduates.

As discussed in the rationale underpinning this collaboration, there is demand from UK employers for information literacy skills in the graduates they employ. The business world is becoming increasingly aware that the ability to use information technology does not equate to effective research skills. Therefore, in the recruitment process, candidates who offer higher-level research skills will have a cost effective impact in the knowledge-driven workplace. The student feedback indicates that students are aware they have improved their skills and see that this will be useful across modules, in placements, and in the world of work:

> These skills should help me not only in other modules at university, but they can also be used collectively in the working world as well.

> These skills developed will be beneficial to both this module and every other research tasks I undertake in university and my professional life.

Ali and Katz (2010: 17) have identified the problem that 'employers seek ICT-literate workers, yet business schools might not be teaching these skills,' and we believe that through our collaboration we have gone some way to addressing this issue in the modules *Managing in a Global Context* and *Globalisation and Business*. Our collaboration has assisted students to gain the research skills which will enable them to become graduates with impact.

References and URLs

Ali, R. & Katz, I. R. (2010) *Information and Communication Technology Literacy: What do businesses expect and what do business schools teach?* [Online]. Princeton: ETS. Accessed 3 February 2010 at http://144.81.87.152/Media/Research/pdf/RR-10-17.pdf

Association of Graduate Recruiters (2010) *Class of 2010 faces uphill struggle for jobs.* [Online] Accessed 7 January 2011 at http://www.agr.org.uk/content/Class-of-2010-Faces-Uphill-Struggle-for-Jobs

Brown C., Murphy T., and Nanny, M. (2003) Turning techno-savvy into info-savvy: authentically integrating information literacy into the college curriculum. *Journal of Academic Librarianship* **29** (6) 386–98

Cheuk, B. (2008) Delivering Business Value through Information Literacy in the Workplace. *Libri* **58** (3) 137–43

De Saulles, M. (2007) Information Literacy amongst UK SMESs: an information policy gap. *Aslib Proceedings* **59** (1) 68–79

Harris, T. G. (1993) The Post-Capitalist Executive: An Interview with Peter F. Drucker. *Harvard Business Review* **71** (3) 114–22

JISC (2009) *Thriving in the 21st century: Learning Literacies for the Digital Age.*[online]. Last accessed 7 January 2010 at: http://caledonianacademy.net/spaces/LLiDA/uploads/Main/LLiDAreportJune09.pdf

Oblinger, D. and Oblinger, J. L. (eds) (2005) *Educating the Net Generation* [Online]. Boulder: Educause. Accessed 7 January 2010 at http://net.educause.edu/ir/library/pdf/pub7101.pdf

Rushton, D., Sparshatt, L. and O'Brien, R. (2010) Feed-Forward: Supporting transferable skills with formative feedback. In Kemp, P., Atfield, R, and Tong, R. (eds.) *Enhancing Learning through assessment in business management hospitality leisure sport tourism.* Newbury, Threshold Press

Sheffield Hallam University (2010) *Sheffield Hallam University Graduate Attributes* [draft 16th June 2010]

DIANE RUSHTON is a senior lecturer in international business at Sheffield Business School. Her research interests are in the area of developing students' research skills, writing skills and student assessment and feedback.

ALISON LAHLAFI is Information Specialist and Team Leader for the Learning and Information Services Team that supports Sheffield Business School staff and students. Research interests include development of staff and student information literacy skills and library support for international students and internationalisation of the curriculum.

ERICA STRETTON is Information Adviser for International Business in the Learning and Information Services Team that supports Sheffield Business School at Sheffield Hallam University. She is interested in active learning in information literacy teaching.

Appendix 1: Assignments and Assessment criteria
Assessment Task 1
Part 1
You are required to research the topic of Globalisation through five on line resources such as:

❏ peer-reviewed journal article
❏ journal article
❏ newspaper
❏ International organisation
❏ pressure group
❏ non-UK/USA site
❏ Government site.

Compare and contrast each website/article and evaluate the credibility of each website.

❏ Accuracy of article/website
❏ Authority of article/website
❏ Objectivity of article/website
❏ Currency of article/website
❏ Coverage/evidence base of the article/website.

This should be produced as a table of key points. You should then write a discursive and analytical commentary of the key issues relating to the above. You should include referenced examples from the articles you have found to illustrate and support the points you are making. 1,500 words.

You must use Harvard referencing.

Part 2
Write a reflective summary (two sides A4) of

A) what you have learnt about the use of the internet as a research tool for this module
B) your own research capabilities and technique and how you will use and develop them through this module

You should include the following, plus any thing else you consider relevant.

❏ ease of use of the online resources
❏ did you just use the directed page or did you explore? Why/ why not?
❏ how easy was it to find supplementary material?
❏ how easy was it to find out information about the author of the article
❏ what is the advantage/disadvantage of using online resources as opposed to books /journals?
❏ how this exercise enhanced your learning in terms of both knowledge and researching?

❑ how will you use what you have learnt about the internet as a resource in your other assessment tasks?

❑ what have you learnt about your research technique?

Assessment Task 2
Report Proposal

You are required to write your report proposal for each of the sections of the final report, as outlined in assessment task three. The purpose of this is so we can give you feedback-feed-forward on your report writing ability and the focus and proposed content of your final report.

   You should include:

❑ The focus of your discussion of globalisation

❑ The global industry sector and briefly explain why you have chosen it in terms of globalisation.

❑ Top ten global companies in your sector and other global key players that have an influence on the industry sector. You should clearly outline the focus of the analytical and critical discussion of your key players for your main report. You must not write a descriptive history of each company

❑ Theories, concepts and key issues, introduced in the lectures and developed in the seminars, you will use and explore in the critical analysis of the impact of globalisation on your industry sector. You must justify why you are focusing on these particular topics.

❑ Specific sources you will use, such as particular journal articles you have found that will support your argument, particular academic textbooks that will help you explain the academic theories, particular company websites that will provide you with company specific material to support your analysis of the industry sector. Do not just say books and internet, you must be specific. This must be produced as a Harvard Reference List and does not constitute part of the word count. You should have a separate Harvard list for this report proposal at the end.

You must include, as an appendix to your report, a detailed outline of your report structure, indicating by numbered sections, the theories, concepts and key issues you will discuss.

   The proposal should be no longer than 2,000 words and in report format. If you are unsure of how to write a report, use the online resources available for guidance and look at some actual business reports. You will be given guidance in the seminar.

   You must use Harvard referencing.

   You must submit your proposal through Turnitin.

Assessment Task 3
Report

For a global industry sector of your choice write a report, 5,000 words, to explain and illustrate the impact of globalisation on that global industry sector.

The report should be factual, discursive and analytical of the module relevant key issues for your particular industry sector.

Your report must:

❑ Demonstrate your understanding of the growth and development of Globalisation

❑ Identify the top ten global companies in your sector and other key players in your industry sector that have influence. You should not write a history of each of the organisations. You should demonstrate and critically comment on the impact of globalisation on them.

Your report must cover four or five of the following module topics relevant to your particular industry sector:

❑ The role of the WTO in your industry

❑ The role of the IMF in your industry (this is limited to only a few industry sectors)

❑ The impact of trading blocs in your industry

❑ The impact/influence of emerging markets in your industry

❑ Globalisation of markets in your industry

❑ Globalisation of production in your industry

❑ Globalisation of outsourcing in your industry

❑ Global joint ventures, strategic alliances in your industry

❑ Ethical and corporate social responsibility issues specific to your industry sector that are a result of globalisation.

You should look at online resources if you do not know how to write a report. Please note a report is NOT an essay with subheadings, it has a specific structure and the headings and numbering have a specific purpose.

You must use Harvard referencing.

You must submit your report through Turnitin. Please remember that it can take up to two days to get the Turnitin report back so ensure work is submitted to allow time to make any necessary adjustments. You can then resubmit your final version.

Assessment criteria

Web-based exercise (Degree students)

	Reflection	Analysis and research	Communication
70% +	Incisive, comprehensive, and evaluative reflection of both (A) and (B), supported by evidence.	Thorough analysis and evaluation of all five websites. Information and conclusions support each other. Coherent conclusions. Flair and originality in research	Relevant professional and academic language enhances meaning. Well structured and cohesive. Referencing is thorough and complete with all sources acknowledged using Harvard system. Accurate bibliography is included.
60% – 69%	Competent and evaluative reflection of both (A) and (B), supported by evidence.	A good standard of analysis and evaluation of all five websites. Coherent conclusions. Full use of research skills.	Conventions of written English sentence structure used to enhance meaning. Well structured and cohesive. Referencing follows Harvard conventions. Accurate Bibliography is included.
50% – 59%	Reflection is realistic and covers a broader range of research skills, supported by evidence.	A good standard of analysis and evaluation of most websites. Conclusions based on research skills.	Grammatically correct written English. Well structured. Referencing follows Harvard conventions. Accurate bibliography is included.
40% –49%	Key research skills identified. Reflection is realistic and covers strengths and weakness supported by evidence.	Patchy analysis and evaluation of identified websites. Partial conclusions. Fundamental research skills demonstrated.	An acceptable level of written English. Has structure. Referencing is incomplete or/and inaccurate. bibliography is inaccurate
Below 40%	Little or no reflection of both (A) and (B) or reflection of only (A) or (B). Little or no supportive evidence.	Weak evaluation and analysis of identified websites. Little evidence of acceptable research skills.	Poorly written with errors in grammar and/or vocabulary. Meaning often obscured. Little structure. Poor or no attempt to reference. Poor or no bibliography.

Proposal (Degree students)

	Research and content	Communication
70% +	The subject matter is highly relevant and is comprehensive. In depth research has been undertaken using wider ranging professionally appropriate research skills.	Relevant professional and academic language enhances meaning. Well structured and cohesive. Referencing is thorough and complete with all sources acknowledged using Harvard. Bibliography is accurate.
60% – 69%	All subject material is directly relevant. A wide and indirect variety of research sources are used.	Conventions of written English sentence structure used to enhance meaning. Well structured and cohesive. Referencing follows Harvard. Accurate bibliography.
50% – 59%	All subject material is directly relevant. A range of differing sources is used effectively.	Grammatically correct written English. Well structured. Referencing follows Harvard. Accurate bibliography.

| 40% – 49% | The majority of the subject matter is directly relevant. Basic research has been done but draws on an obvious set of source materials. | An acceptable level of written English. Has structure. Referencing is incomplete or/and inaccurate. Bibliography is inaccurate. |
| Below 40% | A significant amount of the material is not relevant to the question and/or there are major gaps in coverage. Draws on a very limited set of source materials, some or all of which are irrelevant to the task set. | Poorly written with errors in grammar and/or vocabulary. Meaning often obscured. Little structure and no attempt to reference. No or inaccurate bibliography. |

Report (Degree students)

	Content and theory	**Analysis**	**Research**	**Communication**
70% +	The subject matter is highly relevant and is comprehensive. Broad and deep coverage of theory and concepts, including those from other disciplines.	Thorough analysis of relevant issues Well integrated theory and practice.	In depth research has been undertaken, using a wider ranging professionally appropriate research skill.	Relevant professional and academic language enhances meaning. Well structured and cohesive. Referencing is thorough and complete with all sources acknowledged using Harvard. Accurate bibliography
60% – 69%	All subject material is directly relevant and is used effectively to answer the question.	Comprehensive identification and analysis of issues. Well integrated comparisons of theory and practice.	A wide and indirect variety of research sources are used.	Conventions of written English sentence structure used to enhance meaning. Well structured and cohesive. Referencing follows Harvard. Accurate bibliography.
50% – 59%	A good answer. All subject material is directly relevant. The answer is effective but there is scope for further development in some areas.	Analysis of key issues. Coherent linkage between theory and practice.	A range of differing sources is used effectively.	Grammatically correct written English. Well structured. Referencing follows Harvard. Accurate bibliography.
40% – 49%	The majority of the subject matter is directly relevant. The answer is adequate but there is scope for further development in many areas.	Analysis of some issues. Some linkage of theory and practice.	Basic research has been done but draws on an obvious set of source materials.	An acceptable level of written English. Has structure. Referencing is incomplete or/and inaccurate. Inaccurate bibliography.
below 40%	An inadequate answer. A significant amount of the material is not relevant to the question and/or there are major gaps in coverage.	Little or no attempt at analysis. Few or no comparisons of theory with practice.	Draws on a very limited set of source materials, some or all of which are irrelevant to the task set.	Poorly written with errors in grammar and/or vocabulary. Meaning often obscured. Little structure and no attempt to reference. No or inaccurate bibliography.

16

Formalised student volunteering opportunities – impacts in sport development and coaching

Melissa Anderson, Lucy Wheatley, Mike Wall and Richard Tong
Cardiff School of Sport, University of Wales Institute, Cardiff

This chapter reviews the *Student Volunteering* module
available to students in the Cardiff School of Sport, UWIC
and reflects on the impact of volunteering not only in terms of
enhancing students' key skills and employability, but also the
overarching effect that volunteers and graduates can have
on the partner organisations and the wider community.

Introduction and background

In line with its mission – to deliver high quality, vocationally relevant sport-related courses and produce graduates with the transferable skills that are valued in the modern workplace (UWIC, 2010) – the Cardiff School of Sport (CSS) has adapted and developed the generic UWIC *Student Volunteering* module. This module was initially validated for all UWIC students and delivered by staff from the careers department. It required students to undertake 40 hours of voluntary work in an environment linked to their programme of study.

The key objectives of this module were:

❑ To broaden students' experience
❑ Develop personal and professional skills
❑ Enhance students' employability
❑ Improve students' ability to reflect on and evaluate their skills and knowledge identifying areas of strength and those in need of further development.

In the Cardiff School of Sport the module is compulsory for students of BSc (Hons) Sport Coaching and optional for those enrolled on BSc (Hons) Sport Management, BSc (Hons) Sport Conditioning, Rehabilitation and Massage, BSc (Hons) Sport Development and BSc (Hons) Sport and Physical Education. It regularly attracts approximately 200 students per year. In order to place the students successfully, partnerships have been established with approximately 30 organisations in South Wales. These include schools, local authority sport development units, sports clubs,

Planning, Preparation and Assessment (PPA)[1] cover specialists and national governing bodies[2] (NGBs).

UWIC staff and partner organisations liaise to develop placements suited to achieve these objectives. Students have the opportunity to select one of the placements with a partner organisation or identify and arrange their own placement with an alternative organisation (although alternative placements must fulfil specific criteria to ensure that the learning outcomes of the module are fulfilled).

With the range of degree programmes followed by the students enrolled on the module, a wide range of placements has to be secured, allowing students the opportunity to test their skills in real-life situations, develop a realistic understanding of the workplace and gain experience which will assist in identifying possible career pathways. Key factors which have contributed to the success of the module to date include:

❏ students are required to reflect on key transferable skills (which has encouraged engagement and personal development)
❏ guest lecturers from key sporting organisations such as sports councils and NGBs of sport (which helps to provide authenticity and contextualisation to the module)
❏ building and maintaining relationships with partner organisations.

This module is part of the second year of undergraduate study (Level 5) and students have a formal opportunity to take their experience further by opting to take the CSS *Work Experience* module in Year Three (Level 6).

To evaluate the impact of the module on graduates, the organisations involved and the wider community, representatives from partner organisations were interviewed. These employers have provided voluntary placements since 2007–08 and also offer full-time paid opportunities to graduates who had completed student placements in their organisations. Additionally, former students who gained employment as a direct result of their placement were also interviewed. The interviews focused on skills developed through the placement experience, the impact on students' employability and broader social skills, impacts on partner organisations and areas for improvement. The key findings are discussed in this chapter.

Impact on students

The interviews revealed that increases in the number of sport-related programmes, and in the number of sport graduates over recent years, have increased competition for jobs and improved the standards of applicants; so an entry-level post such as a

---

1   PPA provides teachers with the right to 10% time away from the classroom. This time is allocated to planning, preparation and assessment. It was introduced in 2005 with the aims of raising standards, tackling workloads and improving the work/life balance of teachers in Wales.
2   Each sport in the UK has a national governing body which oversees the management and development of that particular sport. Typically, NGBs are responsible for increasing participation, developing talent and delivering top level success.

5x60 officer[1] reportedly attracts more than 150 applications. The employers interviewed said that there was a real need for sport graduates to 'stand out' from the other applicants by undertaking voluntary and paid-work placements and by 'building up their CV in terms of experience and making themselves more employable'. This was described by the coaching and workforce development officer for one local authority:

> The person specification says relevant degree ... then show us how you've done this, show us how you've done that, give us examples – so that's where experience comes in ... how are you going to make yourself stand out from the person sitting next to you?

Thus the employers and previous students interviewed agreed that 'volunteering is a necessity' to secure graduate level employment. Let's look at the components which contribute to securing employment.

Combining academic theory and practical experience

Students and employers see the *Student Volunteering* module as providing essential 'added value' to the programmes offered at UWIC, as it offers a formal opportunity for students to take up volunteering and encourages those who may not have considered one before. A local-authority-based coaching and workforce development officer emphasised this as she discussed how a number of UWIC students:

> Have had the opportunity to gain experience in a variety of environments including coaching, volunteering, project work and event support ...and have gained practical skills in dealing with the day-to-day issues ... giving them the practical skills to match the theoretical studies in university and allowing them to demonstrate their capabilities within the workplace.

Former students recognised that the combination of academic theory and practical experience is fundamental to employability and professional success as a graduate. They indicated that practical experience is essential in giving a more complete understanding of the theories and policies discussed in lectures. For example, one former student commented that the voluntary placement

> backed up the things being taught in lectures so that all the policies that were being implemented – [he] could go out and see what they were trying to achieve.

One sport development officer also indicated that students often fail to understand the complexities of the 'real world' and that when they are on a placement they are helped to see that

> it's not one boss and one scheme of work ... officers all have different targets and it's about how they marry together.

---

1   5x60 is a Sport Wales scheme which seeks to encourage those young people who do not take part in sport to get active. 5x60 officers are currently working in Welsh secondary schools to extend the extracurricular programme to include activities that young people request.

Key-skills development

The *Student Volunteering* module was endorsed by all employers as a good opportunity for students to develop their key transferable skills. Well developed communication skills, negotiation skills, conflict management skills and the ability to work independently were identified as important for future employment in sport and leisure. In particular, the coaching and workforce development officer said that potential employees must be able to:

> Adapt their communication style to fit who they are dealing with in any organisation ... as you are dealing with volunteers who are students ... you're dealing with volunteers who might be adults ... teachers or parents ... then you're dealing with operational managers, leisure centre managers, chief officers ... one of the biggest assets that they would take away [from a voluntary placement] is being able to differentiate and identify when they need to change their communication style and being able to recognise when a certain style is not working.

All former students recognised the value of this 'hands on' experience in terms of the development of key and transferable skills. One student illustrated this point by stating that the softer skills gained through the coaching experience, such as communication skills, people management and planning skills, helped him greatly in securing a postgraduate voluntary placement.

However, there was also an appreciation that the development of these skills was not only relevant to a career in sport. Indeed, one student said that the placement had enabled him to become a 'more rounded' individual as he could have gone down any employment route and would still have needed teamwork, the ability to work on [his] own and sound communication skills. The coaching and workforce development officer concurred with this and described how these skills were relevant to business, retail, sport development or the teaching profession.

Reflection on the development of key skills is required throughout the module;

Figure 16.1
A Cardiff School of
Sport volunteer in a
coaching role.
(*CSS*)

students are required to complete a reflective log and to liaise with their tutor to identify key areas for further development, to ensure a continued focus on interpersonal skills and personal development. It is important that students not only have a work experience opportunity but that they can demonstrate that they have learned from it and developed key transferable skills, for example, communication and leadership, as a result of this experience. Thus, reflective practice plays a critical part in the module.

Networking and further opportunities

Their experiences in this module also provide students with networking opportunities and key links which are a further platform for additional voluntary work, paid work or training opportunities. Although paid opportunities in sport development and coaching will depend on specific project funding, and may be limited for students who do not hold a NGB Level 2 coaching qualification, in some instances the placement secured as part of this module has led a graduate directly to their first professional position. This benefit was clearly recognised by all of those interviewed, as illustrated by one local-authority sport development officer:

> This is a real opportunity for [students] to get a foot through the door. Traditionally, local authorities have gone to people they know with entry level jobs ... knowing people face-to-face will get [students] a lot further.

One former student interviewed is currently employed as an active young people officer and he indicated that professional relationships developed during his voluntary placement directly helped him secure his first graduate post and have since assisted him in his work:

> The biggest benefit from my volunteering module was networking and creating relationships within [the local authority] sport development team ... They are relationships I built up from scratch and ... I still call upon favours from [those individuals] from time to time in my post.

For students not fortunate enough to secure a full-time paid post following their voluntary placement, all employers said that the successful completion of a placement would provide additional opportunities for voluntary or part-time project work. For example, one employer commented that 'if they do a good job, that's the best thing they can do because they get remembered [and] they get given additional opportunities.'

However, all respondents indicated that the 40 hours of voluntary work required for the module should be considered a bare minimum if students are serious about enhancing their employability. One employer said that the *Student Volunteering* module:

> is like dipping your toe in ... and students need to take the whole plunge ... to really demonstrate to employers that they've got a thorough understanding [because students] that generally 'get on' and get a job will be those who continue and do

half a day per-week for the whole year because they just get more experience …
doing all the hours in one week is not the point of it.

This same employer suggested that the *Student Volunteering* module should require
students to undertake a longer-term placement in excess of 40 hours – and that the
module 'should be mandatory [for any] university looking at making more of their
students employable.' As this is not practical, given the resources available for managing the students, it has been suggested that the module is linked to the Millennium
Volunteers award scheme, which rewards students for undertaking 50, 100 and 150
hours (Wales Council for Voluntary Action, no date). Such a scheme not only allows
students to develop their key employability skills, but actively rewards individuals
for long-term commitments to community-based activities.

In addition to the developing their employability skills, their experience has led
some students to develop a long-term interest in volunteering in sport. This activity
contributes to the provision of sport and physical activity and arguably enhances
graduate impact, builds social capital, broadens horizons and brings people into
contact with those outside of their normal social circle (Coalter, 2007). One of the
students confirmed that the experience had 'created a lifelong interest in coaching
gymnastics' while another said that his 'bank of volunteering has provided a base
level to move on to coaching, leadership or employment' without which he might
not have remained involved in sport. All employers said that a wider involvement in
sport (for example, coaching, attending workshops or volunteering for local clubs)
was essential for a student's employability if they sought a career in either coaching
or development, as it indicated enthusiasm, commitment and initiative.

This research confirms that employability is a key motivational factor for volunteering as placements are able to provide practical opportunities for key-skill development, networking and learning. However, evidence was also available to support
the suggestion that student volunteers can make meaningful contributions to organisations and communities (Brewis et al, 2010). Indeed, Sport England and the Local
Government Association (1999: 8) suggest that:

> voluntary and community activity is fundamental to the development of a
> democratic, socially inclusive society. Voluntary and community groups…..enable
> individuals to contribute to public life and the development of their communities.

Thus, irrespective of whether individuals volunteer for altruistic reasons or otherwise, volunteering appears to be of benefit to both the individual and the community
as a whole.

Impact on partner organisations

Two of the employers interviewed as part of the research represent local authorities
which have long-standing professional relationships with CSS, while another said
that she viewed this module as an opportunity to strengthen links and to develop
a close working relationship. A key reason for involvement in the provision of

placements and a broader involvement in the module (for example, through guest lectures) was the nature of the work in their placement organisations. One employer described this by saying:

> There was no question that we wouldn't be involved in the module because as a sport development team … a big focus of what we do is volunteering, coaching and workforce development … so it's a natural link that we provide an exit route for students to come in and get voluntary placements.

Indeed, the employers identified two key benefits of providing placements for students and other volunteers: increasing organisational resources and the reliance on volunteers to deliver and achieve sport development objectives.

Resources

When placements are carefully planned and co-ordinated, student volunteers are well placed to increase the resources of a department and to enrich and enhance work which is already taking place. Employers indicated that students have the skills to undertake important tasks such as small scale research projects and club audits and generally 'take on tasks which would take quite a bit of time to do … taking some workload off officers, allowing them to work on higher level tasks.'

The delegation of such tasks often requires students to communicate with a range of individuals (such as teachers who may not be interested in sport) and can often move them outside their 'comfort zones', thus testing and further developing their interpersonal skills. In this way, both the placement organisation and the volunteers benefit; two of the employers interviewed considered this to be a real strength of the module.

Volunteers in sport

Volunteering in sport is one of the main areas of voluntary work in the United Kingdom, with up to 6m people participating (Gaskin, 2008). Young people between 16 and 24-years-old are particularly involved in sport volunteering – approximately half of all youth volunteering takes part in sport and physical activity – as it is regarded as an opportunity for personal development (Eley and Kirk, 2002). However, it is also suggested that young people volunteer for social and altruistic reasons (Taylor et al, 2003) and the CSS research confirmed this, revealing that volunteers are considered to be 'invaluable to the work of a sport development team,' as they are regarded as a 'free workforce' and can ensure the sustainability of community based projects.

This is particularly important in terms of providing opportunities for children and young people to participate in sport and physical activity on a regular basis. Sporting organisations often lack funding to pay coaches to achieve an appropriate ratio of adults to children. All employers agreed that volunteers require a wide range of key skills, including the communication skills and versatility required to deliver to different audiences. One sport development officer exemplified this by describing

Figure 16.2
'That's right, you've got
it.' Volunteers coaching
cricket.
(CSS)

how they require individuals who 'can deliver a nice session after school or deliver at 9 o'clock at night, to a street games audience'. The latter might possibly be more challenging, as participants tend to be 'from tougher backgrounds and need a little bit of time invested in them.' Schemes such as *Student Volunteering* provide potential graduates with the opportunity to learn how to be effective in dealing with diverse groups of individuals from a range of backgrounds, thus enhancing their impact on society.

Evidence indicates that volunteers are well placed to act as role models in the community. The Youth Sport Trust (in conjunction with Sport England and Sports Leaders UK) manages and delivers a programme called 'Step into Sport' where children aged between 11 and 19 from schools across England are offered the opportunity to develop skills and gain qualifications. Such programmes are developed in the hope that they will remain involved in sport and act as leaders and role models who can motivate and inspire other young people to participate. It is believed that young people make powerful role models for children and could play a crucial part in helping to increase participation in sport and physical activity (Youth Sports Trust, 2010). One reason is that young volunteers have the capacity to act as role models to younger children and act to bridge the generational gap between child participants and adult coaches (Kay and Bradbury, 2009).

Their research also suggests that volunteers see themselves as role models in their community and thus gain a sense of satisfaction from helping and inspiring others (Kay & Bradbury, 2009). One sport development officer suggested that sport volunteers 'highlight to other people that, with some initiative, [individuals] can positively use their skills to really make a difference' in the community. Another employer expanded on this statement, describing how young volunteers are a crucial part of the workforce as they act as positive role models for younger members of the school or community clubs, demonstrating positive attributes such as turning up on-time for activities, informing someone if they are unable to attend, setting up and packing away activities and respecting other young people and adults' [the development of which can] improve life skills, such as communication and leadership, which can have a positive impact on the community in which [individuals] live and study.

In terms of the types of people who volunteer, the students are considered particularly important for three key reasons. A sport development officer suggested that a number of young people volunteer while at secondary school and complete the Level 2 Sports Leaders Award but become less involved at university. If they can be offered accreditation with a module like *Student Volunteering*, students are encouraged to continue contributing to the delivery of sport and having a positive impact in the community. The next reason why student volunteers are considered valuable is that they may be available at times when those in full time employment are not. For example, individuals are frequently required at 3.30 p.m. to run after school 5x60 sessions. Finally, young volunteers are reported to inspire their peers and younger children to participate in healthy, meaningful activities.

Challenges faced in delivering a formalised volunteering opportunity

Given the diversity of the students enrolled on the module and the challenging learning and teaching objectives, a number of difficulties have been faced. These include:

❏ The intricacies associated with developing autonomous, independent learners and ensuring students meet the identified learning outcomes of the module. One employer identified the potential difficulty of working with a student 'who has not really learned how to use their initiative … as it takes an officer's time to chase them up.' However, the same employer suggested that, based on experience, taking students in 'friendship pairs' may alleviate this problem as students tend to motivate one another and will work together to solve problems, rather than relying on their line manager. In addition, all employers identified the placement as a clear opportunity for students to develop initiative and time management skills.

❏ The difficulties experienced by students in terms of balancing their academic studies, sporting activities, paid work and voluntary placements. The employers interviewed as part of this case study understood the demands placed on students. They also recognised that there was a need for placement organisations to offer a wide range of opportunities, for them to liaise with students and identify their personal aims, but also stressed the need for students to demonstrate initiative and to actively seek out opportunities which will set them apart from the rest of the crowd.

❏ Ensuring that placement organisations are able to provide a rich and realistic experience for the students and that the partnership is of mutual benefit to both the student and the organisation. In a small number of instances during the delivery of the module, students have found their placements to be limited in opportunity. For example, this may include placements where students spend their 40 hours observing others in practice rather than coaching or otherwise making a contribution themselves, or where they have been assisting with the organisation of major events and have been allocated long, mundane tasks.

However, these experiences can be minimised if the placement organisation understands what UWIC expects in terms of student engagement and development. In addition, as one of the employers in the case study revealed, clear communication between the line manager and the student volunteer is crucial in identifying what the students want from the work experience and also what the organisation want to gain. These issues can be clarified through a three-way placement agreement between the institution, the student and the placement organisation. However, it should also be noted that where students have reported that they have not found their placements to be particularly enjoyable, they have often indicated that the experience allowed them to understand the reality of the workplace and the valuable contribution of volunteers.

Conclusions

This chapter has identified one of the ways in which the Cardiff School of Sport is attempting to broaden students' experience, develop personal and professional skills and enhance students' employability, creating graduates with impact. Effectively, the *Student Volunteering* module addresses the ambition of the school to deliver high quality, vocationally relevant sports related courses and in so doing produce graduates with transferable skills valued in the modern workplace (UWIC, 2010). Despite the potential issues associated with the planning, delivery and monitoring a module of this size and scope, it is clear that the benefits are substantial and not only have a positive impact on the students and their employability but also on the partner organisations and the wider community as a whole. In short, enhancing students' employability through volunteering provides a significant opportunity to enhance the graduates' impact on leaving university.

References

Brewis, G., Russell, J. & Holdsworth, C. (2010) *Bursting the Bubble: Students, Volunteering and the Community*. London: Institute for Volunteering Research

Coalter, F. (2007) Sports clubs, social capital and social regeneration: 'ill defined interventions with hard to follow outcomes'? *Sport in Society* **10** (4) 537–59

Eley, D. and Kirk, D. (2002) Developing citizenship through sport: The impact of a sport-based volunteer programme on young sport leaders. *Sport, Education and Society* **7** (2) 151–66

Gaskin, K. (2008) *A winning team? The impacts of volunteers in sport*. London: The Institute for Volunteering Research and Volunteering England

Kay, T. and Bradbury, S. (2009) Youth Sport Volunteering: Developing Social Capital? *Sport, Education and Society* **14** (1) 121–40

Sport England and the Local Government Association (1999) *Best Value through Sport: The Value of*

Sport to Local Authorities. London: Sport England

Taylor, P., Nichols, G., Holmes, K., James, M., Gratton, C., Garrett, R., Kokolakakis, T., Mulder, C. & Kind, L. (2003) *Sports volunteering in England: A report for Sport England.* Sheffield: Leisure Industries Research Centre and London: Sport England

UWIC (2010) *Cardiff School of Sport Vision and Mission Summary.* Cardiff: UWIC

Wales Council for Voluntary Action (no date) *What is Millennium Volunteers?* [online] Available from http://www.wcva.org.uk [accessed 5th Jan 2011]

Youth Sports Trust (2010) *Youngsters from London take a 'Step into sport'.* [online] Available from: http://www.youthsporttrust.org/page/media-news-detail/sis-london/index.html [accessed 5th Jan 2011]

MELISSA ANDERSON is lecturer in sport development at the Cardiff School of Sport, UWIC, and the CSS module leader for *Student Volunteering*. Melissa has been responsible for the development of the generic module to ensure that it is specific to the students in the School and is currently developing a Student Volunteering module specific to CSS. Her research interests include physical activity and older people, barriers to participation and volunteering. Melissa has been involved in several research projects commissioned by the Welsh Assembly Government and Sport Wales, including a three-year evaluation of the WAG Free Swimming Initiative.

MIKE WALL is sport administration manager and part-time lecturer in sport management and development at the Cardiff School of Sport, UWIC. His current teaching role involves the delivery of the *Student Volunteering* module. His research interests include strategic management and organisational change. Mike has been involved in a number of externally funded research projects, including a three-year evaluation of the WAG Free Swimming Initiative.

LUCY WHEATLEY is discipline director of professional development and lecturer in sport development at the Cardiff School of Sport, UWIC. Her research interests include social exclusion, community sport development and student engagement and learning in higher education. Lucy has recently completed several pieces of research in the area of technology-enhanced learning. Specifically, this has involved evaluation of the impact of personal response systems to engage students in large group lectures and also the integration of web-based technology as an alternative means of collaborative group working

RICHARD TONG is the director of learning and teaching and deputy dean in the Cardiff School of Sport at UWIC. He was the sport liaison officer for the HE Academy Subject Centre for Hospitality, Leisure, Sport and Tourism until 2010 and is the chair of the Education and Professional Development Division for the British Association of Sport & Exercise Sciences (BASES). Professor Tong is accredited by BASES specialising in pedagogy and is the moderator champion for learning and teaching for the University of Wales. His research interests and publications are in sports physiology, pedagogy and assessment. He was co-editor of an earlier book in the *Enhancing* series, on assessment.

Glossary

ABDC	Australian Business Deans Council
AGCAS	Association of Graduate Careers Advisory Services
ALTC	Australian Learning and Teaching Council
ASBCI	Association of Suppliers to the British Clothing Industry
ASD	Active Schools Dundee
BAFM	BA (Honours) Fashion Management, London College of Fashion
BASES	British Association of Sport & Exercise Sciences
BIS	Department of Business, Innovation and Skills
BMAF	Business Management, Accounting and Finance subject network
CEO	chief executive officer
CETL	Centre for Excellence in Teaching and Learning
CEWBL	Centre of Excellence for Work Based Learning, Middlesex University
CIPD	Chartered Institute of Personnel and Development
CPD	continuous personal development, continuing professional development
CPLS	Centre for Professional Legal Studies, Law School, University of Strathclyde
CSR	corporate social responsibility
CSS	Cardiff School of Sport
DHLI	Dundee Healthy Living Initiative
DLP	Diploma in Legal Practice, University of Strathclyde
DMU	De Montfort University, Leicester
EMCC	European Mentoring and Coaching Council
EPA	Education Partnerships in Africa
ESEC	Enhancing Student Employability Co-ordination team, HEA
GAP	Growth and Transformation Plan, Ethiopia
GATT	General Agreement on Tariffs and Trade
GDC	Graduate Development Centre, LJMU
GTP	Growth and Transformation Plan, Ethiopia
HEA	Higher Education Academy
HLST	Hospitality, Leisure, Sport and Tourism subject network
HRD	Human Resource Development
HRM	Human Resources Management

ICSC	International Centre for the Study of Coaching, Middlesex University
IDEA	Inter-Disciplinary Ethics Applied CETL, University of Leeds
ITT	Institute of Travel and Tourism, UK
LIS	Learning and Information Services, SHU
LJMU	Liverpool John Moores University
LSS	Law Society of Scotland
MDG	United Nations' Millennium Development Goal
MoFED	Ministry of Finance and Economic Development, Ethiopia
MMUBS	Manchester Metropolitan University Business School
MU	Middlesex University
MUMN	Middlesex University Mentoring Network
NGB(s)	national governing bodies [sport]
OERs	open educational resources
PDP	Personal Development Plan
plcs	public limited companies
PM	Practice Management module, Strathclyde Law School
POST	Paediatric Obesity Service for NHS Tayside
PPA	Planning, Preparation and Assessment
QAA	Quality Assurance Agency
REAP	Re-engineering Assessment Practices project, University of Strathclyde`
SERP	Sport Ethics Research Development Project, University of Leeds
SES	Division of Sport and Exercise Sciences, University of Abertay, Dundee
	Sport and Exercise Science, University of Leeds
SHU	Sheffield Hallam University
SOLO	Biggs & Collis taxonomy [1982] of levels of student outcome
SSDS	Student Support and Development Service, University of Leicester
UAD	University of Abertay, Dundee
UNESCO	United Nations Educational, Social and Cultural Organisation
UUK	Universities UK
UWIC	University of Wales Institute, Cardiff
VLE	virtual-learning environment
WGSN	Fashion forecasting database, www.wgsn.com, 'Worth Global Style Network' (not normally spelt out)
WoW®	The World of Work®, LJMU

Index

Enhancing Learning through Assessment

in Business and Management Hospitality Leisure Sport and Tourism

A valuable resource for academics/teachers committed to improving their learning and teaching, ...the discussion, and in particular the excellent examples of current practice, provides a valuable resource for all those involved in teaching in higher education.

Associate Professor Kim Watty

Graduate School of Business and Economics, University of Melbourne

It will be an inspiration for practitioners who wish to review and enhance their practice.

Margaret Price

Professor in Learning and Assessment, Oxford Brookes University

Edited by Pasty Kemp, Richard Atfield and Richard Tong

Assessment is an important element of higher education for both staff and students. This book is a collection of case studies is written by, and for, academic staff, sharing approaches to learning through assessment in a variety of contexts.

In the fourth volume of the *Enhancing* series of books, Professor Mantz Yorke's introduction focusses on 'Assessing emergent professional expertise'.

Contents

Contributors Linda Allin Jenny Anderson Graham Baker Ian Beattie Lesley Fishwick Sara Garratt Pauline A. Gordon David Griffiths Stylianos Hatzipanagos Ursula S. Hummel Jonathan Lean Jonathan Moizer Jill Mordaunt Rich Neil Rona O'Brien Berry O'Donovan Helen Pokorny Gabriel Reedy Diane Rushton Louise Sparshatt Owen Thomas Richard Tong Kylie Wilson Mantz Yorke

£25.00 (paperback)   234 x 156mm   2010   176 pp   ISBN 978–1–903152–

Enhancing the International Learning Experience

in Business and Management Hospitality Leisure Sport and Tourism

Edited by Richard Atfield and Patsy Kemp

Internationalisation is particularly pertinent for academic communities in the UK and around the world. Chapters range from implementing university-wide 'global perspectives' and assessment strategy through inter-university collaboration and review of programmes to the practicalities of adapting individual modules and developing specific learning activities.

Written by academics involved in international learning and teaching, the chapters offer insight into the successes and the pitfalls of embedding internationalisation into the learning experience for business, hospitality, leisure, sport and tourism students.

Contents

Contributors Jan Bamford Nina Becket Maureen Brookes Jude Carroll Alan Darricotte Judie Gannon Rong Huang Elspeth Jones Patsy Kemp Sandra King Mike Lowe Jacqueline Lynch Rod McColl Mari Jo Pesch Sandie Randall Malcolm Sullivan Angela Vickerstaff Philip Warwick Melanie Weaver Rachel Wicaksono

234 X 156mm   2008   176 pp   ISBN 978–1–903152–23–2

Enhancing
Student-centred Learning
in Business and Management Hospitality Leisure Sport and Tourism

Edited by John Buswell and Nina Becket

Outlines successful approaches in supporting the enhancement of student-centred learning. It embraces the theme of employability covered in the first book in this series and moves on to consider the importance of lifelong learning and the role of higher education in the development of independent, autonomous and self-empowered learners.

The case studies, written by academics, offer a variety of perspectives on student-centred learning while discussing lessons learned along the way. Each case study describes a practice or intervention which sets out to engage students and encourage them to take more responsibility for their learning.

Contents

Contributors Mark Atlay Graham Baker Colin Beard Wendy Beekes Karen Bill Will Bowen Jones Derry Corey Simon Cox Crispin Dale Robert French Louise Grisoni Jacqui Gush Carol Jarvis Christine Keenan Susan Lea Jacqueline Lynch Pru Marriot Dominic Micklewright Mark Moss Sarah Nixon Margaret Page Petia Petrova Peter Robinson Angela Tomkins Dorota Ujma Debra Wale Caitlin Walker

£25.00 (paperback)   234 x 156mm   2009   208 pp   ISBN 978–1–903152–

Enhancing Graduate Employability

in Business and Management Hospitality Leisure Sport and Tourism

Edited by Nina Becket and Patsy Kemp

Employability is an important theme for all higher education institutions. This book will be of value to anyone interested in employability, or involved in curriculum development in higher education. The case studies are written by lecturers from the business, hospitality, leisure, sport & tourism communities, and demonstrate best practice in embedding employability into the curriculum.

Contents

ibutors Gillian Armstrong   Karen Bill   Will Bowen-Jones   Nicola Bullivant   John Buswell
Debra Enzenbacher   Lesley Ferkins   Jenny Fleming   Helen George   Kate Greenan
Jacqui Gush   Helen Higson   David Hind   Graham Holden   Marc Keech
Vanessa Knowles   Bridget Major   Mary Malcolm   Una McMahon-Beattie
Angela Maher   Gudrun Myers   Etta Parkes   Petia Petrova   Sean Power
Gail Thompson   Angela Tomkins   Rob Ward   Dorota Ujma

1-9   246 x 189mm   2006   176 pp   ISBN 1-903152-15-7